Mottainai:

A Journey in Search of the Zero Waste Life

FNR Foundation

Thank you to the people of Japan for their guiding presence in the movement toward less waste.

And to Wangari Maathai (1940-2011), founder of Africa's Green Belt Movement, Nobel Peace Prize laureate, and global advocate for *mottainai.*

CONTENTS

Before You Read

The story you are about to read is a lie.

Well, maybe not a lie, but certainly an exaggeration. A fish tale. A fish tail that grows longer with each telling. Actually, the story is more like a fairy tale. A postmodern allegory about a young man who dramatically changes his life.

A regular guy, Greer Grassi could be you or someone you know. A corporate employee with a nice home, a spiffy car, a moderately successful career and a busy life, he feels an underlying sense of desperation. There's this deep hole deep inside, an emptiness that more stuff cannot fill. It's the kind of emptiness that leads you to try new things. Take risks. Explore. Go on a crazy adventure.

That's the story part of the book. The rest of the book is true. No lie. *Mottainai* is not only a real movement, it's a postmodern philosophy. A way of thinking. A way of life. A real way to live.

As you read, remember the dichotomies. True lies, and real truths—the kind we do not always choose to believe or allow to influence us. Hopefully, the story will resonate for you. Enough so that *mottainai* begins to influence how *you* walk through the world.

* * *

Many thanks to the following people for reading early drafts of this book:

Mel Goss, first reader, best reader;

Jade Bos, for suggestions on how to make the story go *boom*;

and Sumiko Uo, for her generous and informative input on Japan and its people.

One: The Guru Finds You

The traffic clogged, inching along the four lane thoroughfare that led to the turnoff to my office. I cranked up the club music, attempting and failing to rev up my enthusiasm for the day ahead. I was tired of being a corporate drone, tired of the day to day monotony, the sameness of the cubicles, the slow rise up through the ridiculous and outdated hierarchy. But I had no other choice. Four years out of school and my college loans were an anchor that bound me to my fate. Somebody had to stave off the circling sharks, and I seemed to be the only person on the planet who could somehow make that happen. Oh, I had decent income, a nice apartment, a cool car. But sometimes it felt like I was drowning, sucked under by my shallow life.

Another Monday morning, the sun not yet scalding hot, the Florida sky a magnificent shade of springtime blue, yet my mood was dark and gloomy. As the newly departed Prince crooned about purple rain, my engine lights went on. Huh? Then the car sputtered and the engine stalled.

Rolling out from the crawl of commuter traffic, I coasted over to the entryway of a strip mall parking lot and pulled in. I swore silently, then loudly when the engine refused to turn over. No faint roar, no click, nothing. Car was dead. Now I would be late for the meeting with the director of marketing. He had a project lined up for me, one that would most certainly involve too many hours of my time spent doing things I detested.

Okay, so maybe the delay wasn't all bad.

After calling triple A, I texted the office to warn them I didn't know when I would make it in. Then I climbed out and guided the car into the closest parking space. Wiping the perspiration from my brow, I checked my designer watch. I still owed on the wildly impractical impulse purchase, but the flashy Patek impressed the women, so I figured it was worth adding to my debt load. Whatever.

With a sigh of exasperation, I slammed my car door closed and leaned against it. A slight breeze fluttered against my face. The air smelled sweet, as it does in the morning before the traffic smog sets in. I decided it was best not to angst about the time it would take for the tow truck to arrive, so I began screwing around on my phone.

The sun beat down. The lush green fronds of a nearby royal palm tree provided me with a little shade, but not much. Not nearly enough. I could feel the sweat dripping down my back.

"*Mottainai,*" a voice said. "What a waste."

I looked up. The sun was in my eyes. In my work attire, with the requisite long sleeved shirt and dark dress pants, I felt damp all over and a little lightheaded. My mood had devolved from bad to foul. The repair to the car I had big monthly payments on would cost me more money I hadn't yet earned, and my debt load hung over me like a fat black cloud in the perfect sky. A cloud that was doing nothing to keep me cool.

"What did you say?" I asked, scowling. I wasn't up for idle chitchat with sidewalk bums.

A few feet away, the man stood staring at me. He cocked his oversized head and laughed. His voice was high, youthful, but he appeared to be comfortably past fifty. His gray hair was long and thick, his big frame padded with middle-age fat. He was dressed in white, in the kind of suit guys once wore to discothèques. On his long feet were white cotton shoes, the type people wore on boats.

"*Mottainai.* A Japanese word. You are familiar with the language?"

No. Why would I be? Japan was irrelevant. These days it was all about China. The kids I'd gone to school with took Chinese lessons. I'd opted out to study computers and play tournament chess. Now I worked in the IT department of a big company and played chess on my phone whenever the busywork died down.

I dismissed the man. "Sorry, no."

I returned to my phone. I'd been scanning the markets, poring over the financials, looking for ways to make an overnight killing. So far, I had lost four figures from my speculative attempts. Not much in the scheme of things, but equivalent to a month's paycheck for me. I needed a win.

And I thought I could make that happen. I was optimistic I could game the system. Everyone was doing it, and plenty of people had managed to make a lucrative career out of it. I was smart, so why wouldn't I be able to join the ranks of the big winners? Instead of standing in an asphalt lot like some loser, waiting for AAA to tow away

3

my overleveraged luxury vehicle.

"*Mottainai* means many things. In Buddhist thought, *mottainai* is essence. What's important. In Japan, the term is used in directing others to waste nothing. Here, with you, it translates to what a waste. Which is what I see here. And I do not mean the broken down car. I mean you, and your lifestyle."

Huh? Was he still talking?

I looked at him again, tensing up a little. So, what, was this weirdo actually trying to rile me? Was this his way of picking a fight? I wasn't in the mood for fisticuffs or even manly ego banter. I was never in the mood for that kind of sports bar bullshit.

"Say, guy, I'm busy here. Want to move it along?" I ventured. I had him by a good twenty-five years. I'd spent far less time at the all you can eat buffet. What could he do to me? "I got more than I can handle right now. You're distracting me."

He laughed at that, emitting another one of his middle school cheerleader giggles. "You're the one who's distracted. Your whole life is being wasted in distraction. Yet I can tell you are very bright, and highly ambitious. This is why I say it. *Mottainai*."

Moe what? Well, Moe Larry Curly, the guy was some kind of a stooge. Whatever the hell he was on about, I was not interested in hearing it. Maybe the sun was getting to me, the morning heat invading my brain as well as clothing suited for air conditioned sedentary behavior, not outdoor lounging. The stranger had slipped under my skin and my usual placid demeanor was bubbling up to a low boil.

I put away my phone. "Bro, you know zip about my life. So why don't you take your *Miami Vice* suit and your paternal but trite advice for a nice hike to the beach. Okay?"

My spine stiffened when his cheerful smile faded. I had never been in a fight. Verbally, I could hold my own, but physical encounters scared me. I knew I could probably take the guy, but I didn't want to have to try. Plus, I had on a super nice shirt by Ralph Lauren. And pleated slacks from Neiman. No way I wanted to mess up my clothes putting Studio 54 in a headlock.

When he stepped toward me, I froze. My heart sped up and warm sweat coursed down my sides, rivering over my ribs. I slipped off the watch and tucked it in my pocket, prepping myself mentally for the oncoming scuffle. Should I put up my fists or wait for him to make the first pugilist move?

"Take this," he said in a lower voice. "Please." He held out a crisp white business card.

What could I do? I accepted it. My heart was racing like I had a bloodstream full of cocaine, but my hand was rock steady.

When he let go of his card, our eyes met. His were snow cone blue. "Hope to hear from you," he said. Then he nodded knowingly at my car. "Good luck with the vehicle."

I said thanks and watched him walk away, hustling east on the brick sidewalk. He moved lightly for a big man. After calming myself, I returned to the financial news. When I looked up from my phone again, he'd disappeared.

The rest of the day was a fiscal nightmare. Tow truck fee, Uber ride to the office, car repair estimate, it all added up to negative numbers. Also, there was the missed meeting, the lost work time, and the sweat-soaked shirt destined for the dry cleaners. I felt out of sorts, totally off my game all day. Then I had to ping Uber again for a lift home. My car would be in the shop until Thursday.

I skipped dinner and went for a run. The city streets were quiet and shadowed, the moon a bleached half-smile high in the sky. Breathing in the cool night air, I jogged past pastel colored apartment complexes behind thick vegetation. The bright purple bougainvillea were in bloom, pink desert roses and red hibiscus flowers everywhere. Everything so sweet smelling, and in an array of brilliant hues. Embroiled in my useless excuse for a life, I'd somehow missed the colorful arrival of spring.

I was always missing something. I missed out on entire days, sometimes weeks. A month could pass without me noticing the world around me. Was this any way to live?

Moe Larry Curly, I thought to myself. What a waste.

Before bed, I retrieved my shirt from the leather chair I'd tossed it on earlier and added it to the dry cleaning pile, then hung up my wool pants. Something slipped out of a pocket and landed on the floor of my closet. A business card.

I picked it up. *Stop Waste! Mottainai Consulting. Martin Handler, President.*

The area code was local.

I stepped toward the chrome wastebasket to toss it, but something stopped me. Call it instinct, call it fate. Whatever guided my hand, I changed direction and dropped the card in a sock drawer instead. Then I forgot about it for almost a year.

By the time I found the card again, the stock market had tanked and none of my brilliant startup ideas had started up. I'd managed to work my way up one rung of the corporate ladder, but I was as bored there as I had been as an entry level drudge. In fact, I was still a drudge, only now with a senior in the job title and a bump up in the pay. I was spinning my wheels, wasting my time in corporate America. My salary didn't make me happy. It didn't even pay off my debt.

Then, one night while raking through my bureau for enough loose change to cover the tip for a delivery pizza, there it was. Martin's business card. I stared at it. The card, it seemed to be calling out to me.

Mottainai.

The next morning, after a long hot shower and a cup of double-strength coffee, I gave the man a call. Martin, the weird dude in the *Saturday Night Fever* suit. The person who would introduce me to my guru and change the course of my life.

Two: A Different Path

We met at the Fast Ninja for lunch and sat side by side at the bamboo sushi bar. Over green tea and hand rolls, Martin told me about his foundation and the philosophy that underlined everything they did in the world. Financed by private donations, the nonprofit business had been established in South Florida with a mission of public education. Mottainai was working to alert people everywhere to the consequences of their wasteful habits, informing them about the need for a global movement toward sustainability.

I was onboard with that kind of thinking, and hip to the issues. My employer owned numerous product brands including several in the food and agriculture sector. A recent acquisition had been a subsidiary selling high-end machines for industrial and home composting. I had incorporated their products into the company website, a job that required I rewrite descriptions for every listing, so I was familiar.

Yawn.

Of course I did understand the need for increased sustainability. I could see how short-term our thinking was, how wasteful our habits. I wasn't oblivious. However, I didn't practice any of that. I mean, I didn't recycle, nor did I buy secondhand. Certainly I didn't compost my food scraps. Still, I got that it was cool to do stuff like that. So, while Martin talked, I nodded my head in agreement.

By the time he dove into a dish of red bean ice cream, Martin had changed the discourse to one of indoctrination. Now he wanted me to join the movement. "Why don't you visit Japan and learn for yourself about the wisdom of *mottainai*?" he said, his mouth full of dairy.

I'd refused dessert and was about to reject the idea of setting out for Asia. I couldn't just skip out on my job and fly halfway around the globe. I couldn't afford to quit either.

That's when Martin explained that the trip would be salaried.

I set my tiny white tea cup on the granite bar. Martin was a strange man. Today he was dressed in a black silk blouse and baggy black pants that ballooned when he moved his legs. His hair was up top in a man bun. He ate with the gusto of a marathoner. But so what? Maybe the guy was a little eccentric, maybe he was super-rich and bat-shit. Who cared? If the trip paid, I would seriously consider it. Traveling around Japan had to be better than being moored to my desk every day, dulled into a sort of zombie coma.

"What kind of salary?" I asked.

He slurped for a moment, drawing out the suspense. "The trip lasts for three months. During that time, we cover your rent and bills while you're away. Also, we pick up the tab for the round-trip airfare to Tokyo, your room and board in Japan. Plus six hundred a week in auto-deposits."

Chump change, but change nevertheless. I did the math in my head. If I could convince my boss to allow me to take a leave of absence, it might actually be doable. Maybe a change of scenery was exactly what I needed. After all, I reasoned, I could really use something to boost my low morale.

With a sudden start, I realized I was smiling.

Martin set his spoon in the empty bowl, pushed the dish aside, and flashed me a wide grin. "I take that as a yes."

I watched silently as he pulled out a thin leather wallet and whipped out a Gold Card. My smile flagged. "This isn't a sex thing, is it?" I whispered.

He snorted with laughter, slapping me on the back hard enough that I coughed. "Greer, my boy, you have a creative imagination bordering on paranoid. No, Mottainai is a legitimate business. Come back to the office with me so I can introduce you to some of the other employees. All of us have gone through the three month training program in Japan. None of us were forced to remove clothing. Except maybe by the TSA." He giggled.

I mopped my mouth with a linen napkin. Did I really want to travel to a foreign country where I didn't speak the language in order to learn about how the Japanese avoided being as wasteful as most Americans were? No, I surely did not. But a paid trip to Asia had to beat sitting in front of three computer screens nine to five working on complicated software for a faceless conglomerate.

Plus, I needed to make some kind of life change. My spirit had been worn down to a nub by the endless drone of everyday busyness that amounted to literally nothing of real value. So why not grab this bizarre opportunity and just go with it?

I followed Martin's bulk out of the sushi bar and into the harsh glare of the afternoon sun. Snapping on a pair of Tom Ford shades, I asked my host, "Where to?"

He smiled. "It's right down the street. We can walk." Then he hustled ahead. He moved extremely fast. I guessed time was one of the things he did not waste much of.

"I don't have a car," he told me when I caught up to him at the next intersection. We stood side by side, waiting for the traffic light to change. "I don't own a house, either." He glanced at me. "*Mottainai* feels like sacrifice at first. Then it feels like the only way to live."

Right. Already sweating and longing for the efficient air-conditioning of my car, I shared a genial smile of agreement. Whatever the man said, I was on board. Once I got to Asia on his dime, however, I could think and do whatever I wanted.

Or so I thought. But I was wrong about that. About everything, as it turned out.

We headed toward the ocean, crossing the bridge over the Intracoastal. As we single filed above the Waterway, I stared down at the gleaming yachts lined up below us, the people onboard in colorful bathing suits, waiting for the bridge to rise so they could motor out to the Atlantic. Must be nice, I thought, to be that rich.

On the east side of the bridge, Martin turned down a dirt side street. More of an alley than a road, it curved around behind the strip malls that led down to the beach. Several feral cats stared at us as we approached, then skittered into the overgrown cocoplum bushes. Huge seagrape trees arched overhead, providing us with blessed shade. The spot wasn't peaceful, however. The rumble of cars and trucks crossing the steel bridge echoed so loudly that the street itself seemed to tremble.

I had been running for ten years and I was on the track team in high school. But I struggled to keep up with Martin. His legs were long and he double-timed it. He seemed to be able to ease through the humid air, streaming along without breaking a sweat. I wasn't lagging, straggling behind him and panting, but I had to really push. And it showed. My polo shirt was drenched by the time he paused under a bright green awning. When I caught up, he was holding open the glass door so I could enter the nondescript cement block building.

Etched on the outside of the door: *Mottainai.*

The bridge horn blasted, an ear piercing sound. Now the bridge would go up, allowing the tall fishing boats and mega yachts to make their way out to sea. I grimaced at Martin as he closed the door after us.

"Rent is so much cheaper here, under the bridge," he explained.

Sure it was. All you had to do was wear ear plugs and the savings would outweigh the suffering, right? Well, I couldn't see myself enduring lifelong hearing loss after sitting in some musty cubicle in this crummy office, that was for sure. Three months in Asia, then on to bigger and better things, I promised myself.

I followed Martin through the empty reception area furnished with a few metal chairs and a heavy oak desk that reminded me of the ones elementary school teachers once used. The desktop was clean except for an old HP computer from the early 2000s. Wow, what an antique. How could the receptionist take care of business with that old thing?

Maybe Martin wasn't so wealthy after all. Maybe he was simply a kook.

He led me down an uncarpeted hallway past a few closed doors and out into the main work area. Six metal desks were scattered around the brightly lit room, each with a rolling office chair, a desktop computer, and a person either yakking on a cell phone or hacking on a keyboard. The hum was low, the light coming in from tall windows on three of four whitewashed walls. Ceiling fans circulated the warm air. Nobody looked up from their busywork.

I stood behind Martin and scanned the room. Ho hum. The office was as pedestrian as I'd ever seen. The employees were all under thirty and casually dressed. Jeans, shorts, tees and sneakers. The atmosphere of naive intensity reminded me of the college newspaper I'd worked for. I'd written articles on why pot smoking should be legal on college campuses, and how grading in non-major courses should be pass/fail. After we went to press, everyone who worked on the student paper tumbled down to the local pub, where we felt we must drink too much in order to be able to go home with one another for a night of forgettable lovemaking.

I must have sighed because Martin turned to me and said,

"Everyone here has trained in Japan. I'll introduce you, then I have work to do. Stay as long as you wish, but drop by my office on your way out." He pointed back down the hall. "Last door before the reception area."

Then he shook my hand. His grip was powerful, his blue eyes intense.

He turned away and cleared his throat. People stopped what they were doing and the room quieted. "Okay, folks, heads up. I want you to meet Greer Grassi. Please answer his questions. Thanks, guys."

With a quick wave, he headed for his office. Six sets of judgmental eyes skated over me, noting my inappropriate designer clothes, my upscale Italian leather loafers, my pathetic sweaty face. When a pretty young woman stood up and introduced herself, I sort of fell in love with her. Like an abandoned puppy will with the first person to show it any kindness.

Her long thick hair fell to her narrow shoulders like a waterfall of color. Reds, oranges, and streaks of gold. "I'm Grace. I can give you the most up to date info on the training program since I only got back six months ago. That is what you're interested in?"

When I nodded, she pointed to a spare office chair and indicated I should roll it next to hers. While I did this, everyone else returned to work. The silent room filled again with the buzz of low voices and the clicking of keyboards, creating a soothing harmony with the background rumble of tires across the bridge.

I scooted next to Grace and said, "So, how was it over there?"

She smiled at me. Her heart shaped face was pale, spotted with tiny freckles. She looked like the girl next door, the one you want to ask out on a date but are afraid to approach because she seems so pure.

"The training is a nightmare," she said in a whisper. "And Mack, our fearless Japanese leader, is unbearable." She handed me a ceramic coffee cup and indicated the water cooler across the room with her head.

I fetched myself a cup of water and drank it down while returning to my seat. I wasn't sure I wanted to go through with this craziness. What was the point?

But when I sat down again, Grace was smiling at me. She had a nice way about her, a reassuring presence. She touched my hand with her soft fingertips. "The months in Japan are life changing," she told me. "You'll absolutely love it."

Three: On the Way to the Way

Less than four weeks later, I was headed for Fort Lauderdale International Airport where I would catch an early morning JetBlue flight to Boston. I had an afternoon flight out of Logan on Japan Airlines, direct to Tokyo. I had a long day ahead of me. Travel time from Boston was more than thirteen hours.

Talk about *mottainai.*

Grace drove me to the airport and kissed me deeply while we were double parked in front of the terminal. We'd been seeing each other since my first visit to the Mottainai office. I was more than a little in love with her.

But not with the idea of giving up all my favorite things in favor of a life of no waste. Grace, however, had been drinking the Mottainai Kool-Aid. In fact, she was swimming in it, and an irresistible *mottainai* goodness seeped from every pore of her perfect body. I wasn't dazzled by the cult of Martin. But I was high on lovely Grace's aura. That and the leave of absence my boss had so generously granted me. Plus the decent stipend Martin was providing for what sounded like a freewheeling adventure. Adding all of this together, I had more than enough incentive to lure me out of my overpriced apartment and launch me on my journey east.

"Skype me from the hotel," she whispered into my mouth.

I promised her I would. Missing her already but grateful to be getting out of town and away from the soul numbing routine, I hefted my overstuffed duffle bag from the back of her Prius and headed for the terminal. When I glanced back over my shoulder, she was gone.

Passing through the revolving glass doors, I thought about how well we got along. Despite our differences, we were oddly compatible. In bed and out. I hoped nobody else at Mottainai scooped her while I was in the wilds of Japan with some strange old wise man. That would be just my luck.

Buried in my thoughts, I bumped shoulders with an overweight businessman who continued past without a word of apology. Rude bastard. Now for the next humiliation, that is, passing through security. With a deep sigh, I prepared myself for a tedious day of annoyance and discomfort. Americans were a boorish lot, and traveling long distance had become an aggravating chore.

At least I was being paid for it.

As I waited in the snaking line that led to the TSA desks, dragging my duffle along the floor as we inched toward the gruff looking agents and their ticket stampers, I thought about what Martin had advised me about the trip. "Be open to everything that comes your way, and you will not waste a minute of the three months of training."

I got that. Being open was cool. But it went against my natural state of being in the world. By nature, I was a bit of a clam. I was quiet, kept to myself, and avoided opening up with strangers. I didn't like to do a lot of new things—or meet new people. In fact, I wondered as the well-dressed lady in front of me began removing her six-inch heels, why was I headed for the far side of the globe when I'd finally found a woman with whom I could be myself?

My phone buzzed. A text from Grace. *I miss you already.*

I had just enough time to text her back, *I will think of you sleeping in my bed, sigh,* before the more burly of the two beefy TSA agents beckoned me over.

On the flight to Boston, I did just that. Grace tucked under the pale green sheets, sleeping peacefully, her long colorful hair streaming across the pillows. I had convinced her to stay at my place while I was gone. After all, Martin would be paying the rent and my luxury high rise was way better than her dumpy house share. The location was much better, too, not too far from the beach and significantly closer to the Mottainai office. But I'd had to talk her into it. She told me my lifestyle was too comfortable, and much too wasteful.

"But if nobody is living there for three whole months, that's a huge waste," I countered.

She had to agree with me there.

With closed eyes, I imagined her fixing a single serving coffee, basking in the steaming hot dual-head shower, and sitting on the patio watching the aerobics class being conducted in the Olympic pool. The images were too intoxicating. I didn't know how I could survive ninety days apart, especially since I would be slaving away on a dirt farm in rural Japan with an ancient farmer.

But in order to impress the woman of my dreams, and to be able to remain the man in her life, that was exactly what I was about to do. After that, I would go back to work with a new attitude. Eventually, I would make my way to the top rungs of the ladder and kill it as a corporate exec. At least, that was what I had told my boss. Time away to clear my head, that was all. A career gap, which some companies encourage for the resulting boost in employee morale and productivity.

I woke up when the captain announced we were beginning the descent. My seatmates clicked off their laptops and buckled their seatbelts. The sky was dark, cloudy, the landing bumpy. We deplaned amidst loud bursts of thunder.

Predictably, my flight out was delayed due to the inclement weather. New England was like that. I'd grown up there, so I wasn't surprised. My childhood had been spent in coastal Maine, where summer lasted from the first week of July to the end of August. The rest of the year it was rainy, cold, or ridiculously snowy. College at BU and grad school in western Mass were more of the same. Which may explain why I jumped when a recruiter called with a job possibility at a Fortune 500 company located in South Florida.

"Every day's a beach day," the guy on the phone informed me.

I'd looked out my apartment window at a foot of dirty snow blocking the icy driveway. "Sounds good," I told the headhunter. "Can you send me the application form?"

When I moved to the sunshine state and started the new job,

the weather had been a delightful change. The natural beauty of the area was astounding, the lush vegetation, gorgeous sky, abundance of wildlife. But the year-round access to nature was one of the few aspects of living in Florida I found fulfilling. And eventually my dulled routine numbed me to that too.

After wandering the terminal and thumbing through glossy magazines in the shops, I buried myself in the Japan travel guidebooks I'd found a few days earlier. I stopped reading every now and again to check the departure board for updates and to purchase coffee refills. As the afternoon dragged on, I gorged on two cheeseburgers and, later, a lukewarm bean burrito. Grace had warned me to get my fill of the things I liked to eat because the training period would not include my kind of food.

"You'll see," she told me on our first date. She'd agreed to meet me for dinner on Las Olas, so I introduced her to my favorite Italian bistro. "You won't be eating pasta, drinking good wine like this, or dining in restaurants, you know." She smiled at me and took a small sip of the Barolo I'd ordered. "Gosh, this is good."

I grinned. Who said words like gosh these days? It was all *shit*, and *goddam it,* and worse. "Will I be living on white rice and grubs?" I teased.

She laughed. "Not exactly. I'm not going to spoil it for you and tell you all the details. But I will say this: the food is possibly the toughest part of the training. That, and the loneliness." She glanced down at her lap, then up again to meet my eyes. "For me, that was the worst thing. I coped well with the other stuff, but..." She shrugged. The smooth freckled skin of her shoulder shone in the candlelight. She wore a simple sleeveless tee with a pair of tight black leggings, the casual outfit adorable, and somehow wildly sexy. I was badly smitten.

Reaching for my wine, I said, "The food will probably be harder for me to adapt to. I like being alone. I thrive on it, actually." When she cocked her head, I shrugged. "I'm an introvert, and kind of an amateur philosopher. I like being in my own head."

She smiled. "Then you'll love the training. You'll be alone most of the time. And with nothing to distract you but whatever is in your own head."

I forked a bite of my eggplant parmesan and held it out for her. "Try this. It's awesome."

While I fed her the mouthful, she brushed my hand with her smooth fingers. I knew I would sleep with her, but not that night. And when I did, when we did, it would mean something.

I'd been right about that. And yet, I was about to embark on a plane flight that would take me thousands of miles away from her.

Mottainai.

The heavy rain eventually let up long enough for my flight to get clearance to depart. Bored and restless, I somehow nodded off to sleep, and managed to remain unconscious for most of the flight.

When we landed in Tokyo, I awoke with a start. Where the heck was I? I was completely out of it. I had no idea what day it was, what time of day—or night.

Outside the terminal, sleek black taxis lined up under heavy storm clouds. From one gloomy sky to the next, I thought as I waited in the short line for my cab. It felt like the same sky as in Boston, but with a completely different backdrop. And South Florida was like another planet altogether. A very distant planet.

The young cab driver turned to me as I slid into the back seat of his car. The leather interior was pristine, and he was dressed in a uniform of sorts with a visored cap and white gloves. Wow. Nothing like taking Uber back home. Sometimes you got a classic muscle car with dice hanging from the rear view mirror, other times a two-seater with little room for your luggage. And nobody wore white gloves.

He said something unintelligible. I shrugged and responded with "Tokyo Tower International Hotel, please."

His dark eyes widened. "You American?"

People were often surprised when they learned that. My father's mother was Vietnamese, my mother's mother from Sioux descent. So I am a real live mixed breed, dark and kind of unidentifiable. I wear my hair long and I think that makes me look like I'm from the Pacific islands. I've been told that, and women often say I look exotic.

Sometimes I've gotten lucky because of that.

"Yup," I said. "You speak English?"

He chuckled. "Yes. We learn in school. You don't speak Japanese?"

I said no. He turned to face the road, waiting for an opening in the traffic stream. Easing into the flow of cars, he began peppering me with questions while darting in and out of the fast moving lanes. "You live in New York?"

When I said no, he said, "You have lots of hot girlfriends?"

Not one to disappoint, I agreed. But to add a dash of truth, I said, "My current girlfriend is a real fox."

He nodded happily. "I want to go to New York. Women so hot there."

We got along famously. He advised me to visit the clubs he called "soap land" where paid guests are given a hot bath by sexy women. He said they catered to *gaijin* there. Foreigners. I assured him I wouldn't miss it, but I only said that to please him. He seemed satisfied when he dropped me at the hotel entrance. He even refused the tip.

What I did not realize was that you don't tip taxi drivers in Japan. Still, I stood before the automatic glass doors of the hotel feeling welcome in a strange city.

The hotel was a steel and glass high rise. On either side, a complex mix of old looking structures, quaint little shops, and modern office towers.

Duffle bag in tow, I made my way into the hotel lobby, a high-ceilinged room that sparkled with white marble and crystal chandeliers. Check-in was conducted in perfect English. *Thank you, sir. I hope you enjoy your stay with us, sir. Let us know if there is anything you need, sir.* I felt stupid. Like an ignorant American who expects everyone else to speak English, even when he's on their turf.

The room was awfully small for the exorbitant fee Martin had paid for my brief stay in Tokyo. All-white walls adorned with miniature watercolors, a soft white duvet on a tidy bed. Sophisticated, elegant, minimalist, and claustrophobically tiny. Fortunately, I wouldn't be there for long.

The room overlooked the crowded street ten stories below. When I opened the window to let in the fresh air, the honking cars and sidewalk bustle were so loud I had to shut it again. The rain had cleared and what looked like early morning sun was attempting to take over a lightening sky.

Propping myself up on the bed, I set up my iPad and pinged Grace. The wireless connection was excellent. She appeared on my screen, smiling, looking almost as beautiful as she had in the early morning light of my bedroom.

"Why aren't you at soap land being treated for jet lag like all the normal *gaijin*?" she joked.

"Ha ha. I guess I'm not that normal," I said. I studied the blank wall behind her lovely head. "Are you at the office?"

She nodded. "It's late so everyone else is gone." She paused.

"It's weird, going back to your place without you there."

"Don't back out on me, now, Gracie. I'm here doing what you think I need to do. So you have to stay at my place for a while, treat yourself a little. We both need to move in the other's direction, right?"

This was my philosophy, not hers. She thought I needed to dump my ingrained materialism in favor of saving the world from mounting heaps of garbage. I wasn't at all sure that was my job.

She shrugged. "I'm not ditching our plan. It's just going to be lonely at your place, that's all."

She glanced away, embarrassed. I wished I could hold her, reassure her everything would be fine. She was used to living in a house full of hippies, hipsters, and PC fascists. I was hoping to ease her into a more adult lifestyle. Couldn't we compromise, make a go of it without having to give it all up for the cause?

Grace changed the subject, sharing the latest updates from the office. I told her about the long layover at Logan, the uneventful flight, and the amusing cabbie. She laughed at my stories, her pretty face flushed with interest, providing the best kind of audience any guy could hope for.

We gushed a bit, making promises and flashing bedroom eyes at one another before saying good night.

"Have fun in the city," she said. "The time you have there will go by fast, so try to see as much as you can before you have to catch the train."

I said I would, and we agreed to talk again soon.

When I clicked off, I had a heavy feeling in my heart. I lay on top of the very firm mattress, and tried to chill. I dozed for a while, my dreams fleeting, disturbing. Grace came and went, always just out of reach.

Four: Rude Arrival

At home, the Memorial Day festivities were in full swing. Barbecues, fireworks, hot dogs and cold beer. Small town parades, live bands in the parks, beaches packed with oiled bodies soaking up sun.

In Tokyo, it was just another day. Yet the atmosphere felt celebratory. Throngs of people surged down the city streets, where everything one could imagine was available for sale. Still groggy with jet lag, I mingled with the international crowd, wandering from block to block. I stopped to enjoy a bowl of udon noodles, and again for a plate of fresh sushi. Both times I was treated to a free pot of tea. In between, I window shopped at the high end luxury stores in buildings the size of New York's tallest skyscrapers. At tiny markets, I bought weird looking fruits that tasted surprisingly good, and nibbled on chocolate-covered soybeans that tasted, well, interesting. Everyone I interacted with seemed happy to help the wandering *gaijin.* The Japanese people were reserved but also exceedingly respectful of others. A delightful change from the rude narcissism that is the hallmark of South Florida.

When night fell, I stopped for a beer at a well-lit bar. While I sipped my glass of Sapporo, I was politely ignored by the other bar patrons, but that was fine with me. As I watched the sharply dressed businessmen who sat in clusters in the leather booths, drinking and conversing, I imagined they were still talking shop. That made me realize how much I did not miss my corporate life.

Kanpai! Cheers.

Back at the hotel, I opened the window again. While I lay on the bed resting my tired legs, the consumer chaos below me continued. It all seemed a bit silly. Wasteful, even.

I sent Grace a text message. *City is incredibly crowded yet people are still polite. Amazing. Food's great. Miss you.*

Early the next morning, still groggy from jet lag, I checked out of the hotel. Bag strapped to my shoulder, I walked the few blocks to the station, where I caught the Hayabusa bullet train to Aomori Prefecture. I was headed for the most northern section of the main island, an area far less populated, home to mostly farmers and fishermen.

The car was packed with commuters and travelers sitting silently in the ultra-modern seats. A few teenagers searched the car with guilty eyes, like they might be playing hooky, but everyone else was busy on their devices. The only sound was the shriek of the fast-moving train. Outside the window, glass skyscrapers sat side by side with low brick buildings and wood houses, and every few blocks I would see green spaces with park benches, playing fields, and mature trees.

Stop after stop, the car gradually thinned out. The passengers disembarked until it was only half-full. Except for me, everyone in the car was much older and Japanese. No obvious tourists.

I read a little and dozed. The three hours passed quickly.

On the platform in the city of Aomori, I waited for a local train. The one I needed would not arrive for a few hours, so I had time to kill.

Mottainai. Grace had instructed me never to say I *killed time*. Our time on this earth is precious, she told me, and must not be wasted.

Hokey stuff, but I had to admit she was right.

I wandered inside the station, which was empty, and purchased a can of tea from a vending machine. Then I sat down and skimmed a tourist brochure from the plastic seat beside mine. The color photos depicted popular sites in the prefecture. Apparently, there was a giant Buddha statue that was considered worth seeing. Also, a castle. Shipwreck Beach on Mutsu Bay, which wasn't too far from where the farm was located, had wild horses. I could go for that, horses galloping across the sand would be worth seeing. There was also a landmark of sorts, a grave that some claimed belonged to Jesus. Rumor was the great man had escaped his fate in the Middle East and fled to rural Japan, where he married and raised a family. Who knew?

The afternoon sun was high in the sky, but the temperature was not the least bit warm. Even waiting inside the heated station, my cold-sensitive Florida-weathered bones felt chilled. Eventually I wandered back outside and paced the platform along the tracks, warming up. Summer in Florida was long, hot, humid, and tedious. But right then, I was wondering if I was about to spend the next few months wishing I was back there.

The station itself sat in the midst of thick woods. Scrutinizing the trees, I recognized the Japanese cypress called *hiba*, plus Japanese red pine. There were numerous stands of beautiful beech trees. The forest stretched into the distance where the mountains were white with snow.

When the train pulled in, the sky had darkened to a purplish blue. I was the only person boarding the small rail car, and most of the seats were empty. The trip to Fukamura wasn't long, but this particular line was not as fast as the bullet train. It would be pitch black when I arrived at my destination. In Florida, there is so much light pollution it's never really dark. I doubted that would be the case in this part of Japan.

It wasn't. The darkness deepened as the train rushed farther into the countryside. When we climbed into the mountains, the air grew colder. I watched out the window for signs of life. The tracks passed the occasional small home, the windows always dark. No cars zooming up driveways, no rowdies hosting parties, no blue glow emanating from giant TV screens. The landscape made me think nothing here had changed in the past hundred years.

Of course, that was not the case. Still, the scenery created a quiet sense of peace that felt exceedingly foreign.

At each stop, I scoured the platform, trying to get a look at the residents of this faraway place. The few people I saw looked like locals, farmers and homemakers. There wasn't a business suit or a laptop bag in sight. No cameras or travel luggage, either.

At some point, I nodded off, awakening with a start. The train was stopped so I glanced out the window. A block letter sign hung above the platform. *Fukamura.*

Yikes!

Grabbing my duffle bag, I hurried down the aisle and out the open doors. Then I stood on the platform. The air was biting cold, and fresh snow dusted the ground.

The train took off, heading to some other small Japanese town. The silence settled in around me, muffling like a snow storm.

I was alone, and it was dark, and, my god, was it cold.

With a shiver, I pulled out my phone. To make sure, I emailed, texted, and called my host, leaving the same message each time. *I am here, please come get me.*

There wasn't much else I could do so I waited. The trees were even thicker here, a dark mass of impenetrable woods that formed a tall fence on either side of the train tracks. I tucked my bag under the bench and paced up and down the deserted platform, trying to stay warm. Eventually he would come, I told myself. Hopefully, I would not be eaten by wolves or mugged by ghostly ninjas in the meantime.

At that point, I knew very little about my host, the cofounder of Mottainai. I'd seen lots of photos of him and his farm posted around the office, and Martin had said he was a fascinating man, a genius and a spiritual person with a generous heart. A philosopher king, Martin said.

But Grace had supplied a few of the more pertinent shadings. Like how he would make you wait for everything until you thought you might burst from impatience, then he'd just laugh at you. *"Gaman,"* she instructed. "Endure." She told me how he grew incredible vegetables and maintained a vast orchard of the most delicious Fuji apples, but subsisted on a meager diet of yams, miso soup, fresh garlic, and burdock tea. Which made me think he was a tease and an ascetic. He sure didn't sound like much fun.

I hadn't been able to find out too much more about Mack, not even after several long nights of determined internet research. I didn't know where he was born, how old he was, or whether he had any family. Nobody seemed to know his birth name. He'd appeared out of nowhere in the mid-1970s, and he looked like an old man even then. He'd burst into the media spotlight after an international hippie commune began battling him over what they saw as their squatters' rights. The case got a lot of attention in the news because the hippies were accused of being some kind of cult.

They weren't, and soon enough they made a bizarre public turnaround. The hippie farmers dropped their lawsuit, instead praising Mack's pioneering work in agriculture. They talked about his unusual farming methods and took his teachings—with Mack's permission— back to their home countries. The enthusiastic young farmers applied what they had learned from Mack, spreading his strange wisdom to small farms in Denmark, Finland, Hawaii, and Iowa. These farms eventually boasted surprising yields of oversized, delicious produce, all grown organically and with minimal farmer inputs.

In some circles, Mack became a kind of agricultural cult figure. Throughout the eighties and nineties, a stream of wannabe organic farmers came to his farm to learn from him. His farming methods were copied, his pithy comments quoted in the alternative press. In this way, the reclusive farmer became an unlikely guru.

I read several studies published in agricultural journals about Mack's farming methodology. His methods were unconventional, but his interview comments were hilarious. He sounded like Charlie Sheen with a twist of Zen master wisdom.

When he fell out of the limelight, as all fads must, the number of sycophants sitting at the great leader's feet, awaiting his pearls of fresh and profane wisdom, dwindled. That's when Martin stepped in and took advantage of the lull in popularity.

Martin had made his first trek to the farm outside Fukamura in 2005, he told me, after reading an old article in an agriculture journal while researching the issue of food waste. He said he found his time with Mack so inspirational, he asked if they might team up to do good work. Mack had agreed to the joint project, and began hosting the young people referred by Martin for training at the farm.

For more than ten years, Martin had sent a steady stream of trainees to spend time on Mack's farm. Some made it through the three months, others dropped out after a few weeks, quite a few only lasted a day or two. This was not reassuring. I was a wimpy American, used to my creature comforts, my blood thinned from the years of temperate living in balmy Florida. I was spoiled, a teacup. Could I hack real life?

Grace had warned how Mack would immediately assign me the chore of cleaning the outhouse (natural composting toilets) and the barn (several goats, a cow, and an old mule, making for a good amount of manure). She insisted it was kind of fun. A girl from Minnesota might find that kind of thing enjoyable, but I couldn't imagine that I would.

Understandably, as I paced the tracks in the middle of the night in the middle of the woods, about to meet this unusual stranger, I had more than a little trepidation. I distracted myself with incessant movement, my breath steaming in the cold night air. The darkness was a thick blanket that surrounded me, threatening to smother me with nothingness. I flinched when an owl hooted, then watched as it swooped down from a tree branch, scooping some poor rodent from the crest of a snow bank.

Nature was harsh, yet somehow just.

This was not a reassuring thought.

I shivered in my wool jacket. Even with leather gloves, my hands were stiff with cold when I fumbled to check my phone. The battery was low. There was no signal now. It had been an hour since I'd messaged and still no sign of Mack.

Great. Just great.

By the time the electric golf cart sped into the station parking lot, I was more angry than cold. Sputtering and swearing under my breath, I grabbed my damp bag and slung it over my shoulder, then jogged over to where the driver had pulled up. He looked tiny, buried in a swath of thickly layered clothing, a ratty scarf wrapped tightly around the lower part of his face. His eyes gleamed from his small face, shiny black and full of life.

"Mack?" I asked.

Who else would it be?

He giggled. I recognized that laugh. Had Martin picked it up from his guru? This really pissed me off. The joke was on me, I guessed. Ha ha.

"Get in," he said. "Middle of night."

No kidding. But he glared at me then. Like my inopportune arrival time was by my choosing and not because he lived in the middle of freaking nowhere.

With a huge sigh, I tossed my duffle in the back of the cart and hoisted myself inside.

Mack floored it and we sped out of the small lot. He didn't say a word after that and I was unable to. Icy air slapped my face until I couldn't even move my lips. My eyeballs felt frozen in place, staring ahead into the wind tunnel of blackness. I hoped the drive was going to be a short trip because, if it wasn't, I was sure I wouldn't survive it.

Gaman, I told myself.

The farm was miles away, the ride there increasingly uncomfortable after we left the main street and bumped along on the badly rutted roadways. Mack turned here and there, the route a dark cold maze. If I needed to leave the training program on my own, I realized, I wouldn't be able to find my way back to the station. Not if I couldn't get a cell signal.

Worries and fears spun around in my mind like dirty clothes in a washing machine. After a while, my brain froze up.

Five: How Not to Spend Your Summer Vacation

I didn't defrost until the next day, when I awoke in the stream of sunlight pouring in the window above my head. My body felt bruised, the futon hard as the wood floor beneath it. I don't know how I slept. My body had been a block of ice, my brain a popsicle.

But now that the sun was out, the small room felt warmer. I guessed I would be spending my time at the farm functioning in the outdoor temperature range, whatever that might be. Yes, it was summer in Japan. But in the northern part of the main island, the weather remained cool year round. And, apparently, frigging cold at night.

When I cracked open the windows, I could smell brine. The Sea of Japan was somewhere in the distance, blowing a clammy scent my way.

Using the supplies I found on a raw wood shelf, I made myself a cup of hot tea. First I had to boil water. There was some in a glass pitcher, so I poured it into a tin pot and set that on top of the one-ring kerosene stove. The kind of stove you use after a natural disaster.

This thought did not cheer me.

I was dying for interior warmth and a solid caffeine kick. The available tea did not come in a bag, however, but was kept in a small jar labeled in Japanese. Steeping the loose tea resulted in a cup of hot water with bitter twigs floating around in it. But maybe I was making it wrong. I'd never been of much use in the kitchen.

Not that there was an actual kitchen in the eight by eight foot cabin where, apparently, I would be spending my summer. There was no refrigerator, no real stove, no cabinets filled with dishware, no pantry full of tasty convenience foods. But I hadn't expected there to be. Grace and Martin had both told me it would be Spartan living. I got that. Still, the rustic scale of my temporary lifestyle was much higher than anticipated. No chair, no desk, no running water, no electricity. Possibly no cell phone.

How would I communicate with Grace? And where would I take a shower? Or *would* I take a shower?

After my terrible tea, which had a flavor something like I imagined a boiled bird's nest might taste, I ventured outside to track down my host. Perhaps he would feed me before sending me to the latrine with a giggle and a scrub brush.

The air was cool but pleasant, the brine lifted away by a sweeter breeze. And the view was absolutely astounding. Snowcapped mountains loomed overhead, impossibly tall and serene. Clouds wrapped themselves around the jagged peaks like loose shawls of misty gray.

The farm consisted of two small wood houses (although where I was staying was more like a hut), an outhouse, and a dilapidated barn. The buildings sat uphill from a sweep of cleared land, with each side ending at thick forest. The far end of the farmland led into a deep stretch of bare trees. The orchard, not yet ripe with apples.

Songbirds filled the air with a delightful sound. Fat bees buzzed past me in the dazzling sunlight. I felt giddy. The place was nothing like the farms people had in Maine. Not like the ones I had seen around the rest of the US, nor any I'd seen in movies or books. The crops were a haphazard array of wild growth intermixed with tall green weeds. This farm was untamed, remarkably beautiful in its natural state, a state of almost primitive wildness.

I sucked in my breath. Wow.

A low voice boomed from behind me. "You need take dump?"

I spun around. He stood on a dirt path that led to the other, much bigger cabin. Where had all the "seekers" stayed when they came to learn from the guru? Had they camped out on the hard cold ground, freezing and suffering, just so they could spend time with this crude little man?

This seemed so pathetic.

"Morning," I said. "What's up for today?"

He cocked his head and frowned. Then he turned around and hurried off.

Okay. Whatever. I followed him, rushing to keep up. For such a small guy, he moved incredibly fast. Again I wondered whether the trait had been copied by Martin. Waste not, walk not?

As we passed through the back yard for my host's house, I shed my wool sweater, draping it on a clothesline strung between two saplings. We didn't head inside his place for a nice breakfast, however, but continued along the grassy path to the barn. As we approached, I heard the cow lowing and smelled the musty aroma of farm animals.

My stomach growling uncomfortably, I followed him inside the tumbledown building. After my eyes adjusted to the darkness, I walked over to where Mack stood petting a small tan cow.

"She likes it when you touch her in the morning. Like a whore," he said.

I didn't know what to say, so I said nothing. I mean, what *do* you say to that?

He pointed to a far wall. "Shovel. You clean stall while I milk."

Okay.

Mack pulled up a three legged stool and went to work. He talked quietly to the cow while he milked her and, I swear to you, she got this saucy smile on her face.

I passed by a stall where the mule stood, tail twitching. He glanced at me idly, then looked away. He was all ribs, ancient looking. I grabbed the heavy shovel and entered the cow's stall. The manure didn't smell bad and it was neat, easy to lift and toss in a bucket. When I finished the job, I brought the shovel and bucket with me to where Mack was sitting.

The pail at his feet was full of steaming milk. It frothed, creamy and rich. I wanted to slurp it up.

"Use cow patty in garden. Not like *your* shit." He didn't look at me when he made this comment. "Your shit go in hole in ground."

Not yet, it hadn't. And it wouldn't if I didn't have a decent meal now and again.

"Do I have more chores before breakfast?" I hinted, trailing behind him as he led the cow out of the barn.

He patted her flank and she wandered off, nose to the ground, munching grass. "Next, we scatter scat. Then clean outhouse. Then eat." He reached for my pail, handing me his.

I left the milk pail by his front door where he indicated, and followed him out to the garden. As he tossed the manure (using his bare hands, no less), a herd of small goats ran up, nudging him with their bony heads. He fed them corn kernels scooped from the pockets of his torn pants. Occasionally, they got excited and pooped right where they stood. This appeared to be part of his ingenious method for fertilizing the gardens.

He led me and the goats around the fields, feeding them and proudly pointing out the various crops. I wasn't sure how he could tell what was what. There were no beds, everything growing together in a mangled mesh of plants and weeds. "Onion. Pole bean. Kale. Sweet potato, yam. Purple one very good for health. Garlic good too. Daikon radish. Rutabaga. Burdock root. Corn."

41

The talk of food had sent my empty stomach into conniptions, and now it was kicking and screaming. I would have to get prepared from now on, pick myself some ripe veggies to eat before the day's work began. I was already exhausted. I couldn't go hungry like this and expect my energy to last through the morning.

When we reached the far end of the garden and stood before the naked apple trees, Mack looked especially peacocky. "Very hard start orchard. Take many years. Most tree die. But now I grow Sun Fuji, best apple in Japan. You see later. Everyone love my Fuji apple."

The skinny branches appeared to be barren, but when I looked closely I could see tiny pale buds. I couldn't believe I would still be here with this strange man when the trees were in full bloom, branches leafy and green, heavy with ripe red apples. Sweet, juicy apples.

My empty belly let out a loud roar of desire.

Mack turned to look at me in surprise. His dark eyes sparkled when he laughed. "Maybe fix breakfast first. Clean outhouse after."

I may have had tears in my eyes when I thanked him. He snorted, then hurried back toward his house, a smattering of the goats trotting behind. They scattered at the doorway, scurrying away after Mack clapped his hands, then ducked inside. I stood outside, waiting politely to be invited in.

"Bring milk," was my welcome to my host's humble home.

I lifted the pail, the contents still bubbly and warm. I am not big on dairy foods due to lactose intolerance, but the fresh milk smelled heavenly. I lugged it over to a low wood table on the far side of the room. But Mack stopped me and pointed to the polished wood floor, so I set it there.

His place was so much nicer than the dreary hut I was staying in. But of course it was, I reminded myself, the man lived here.

I wandered around. There were several rooms, each furnished with modern amenities. A glass desk in one corner of the living area held a laptop and a long-necked table lamp. There was a thick wool throw rug by the wood stove and lovely framed etchings on the pastel walls. In the kitchen, a stainless steel fridge, cutting boards on hardwood counters, and a stove cluttered with pots and pans of various sizes. And an electric rice cooker.

He had electricity? Of course he did. Otherwise, how would he be able to operate his golf cart?

So why the dark dirt hut for visitors?

He read my mind. "You start with basic. I had to do when I first come to build farm. After time pass, you get more extra thing. Appreciate luxury that way. Learn not to waste."

I nodded, wondering if he would let me charge my phone. Was there cell tower access or not?

He handed me a sharp knife and pointed to the kitchen counter. "I give you onion, green bean, goat cheese, and you chop. I make good omelet. Fresh egg from neighbor farm."

Neighbors? Somehow this surprised me. It felt like we were alone on Mack's planet. As I chopped the veggies into bite-size pieces, I wondered how far away the folks with chickens lived. Would we socialize, have parties and potluck dinners? I doubted it.

Mack had been right, his omelet was magnificent. Or maybe I was just starving. The rice he served also tasted delicious, and I can't say enough about the coffee. He used a grinder for the beans, and a small French roast coffee maker. He made me a big cup of café au lait with the fresh milk. It was heavenly.

We sat across from one another on big floor pillows. The low table between us was a *kotatsu*, a special Japanese table made with an electric heater underneath to keep diners warm. Another amenity I hoped I'd be invited to share with my host.

While I shoveled in the food and drink, he sipped from a large mug of brown tea. When I asked if he wanted some of the omelet, the fluffy rice, the delightful coffee, he shook his head. "Today you eat like king. After long journey, before next journey. Journey to learn *mottainai*. Tomorrow, you begin. Farm what you eat, eat what you farm."

Darn. I'd begun to fantasize about Mack serving as my personal chef for the summer. Now my mind turned to goat poop and pricker-weed stir-fry. I set my lacquered chopsticks next to the ceramic plate and picked up the mug of coffee.

"Tell me what you will want me to do this summer," I said.

Mack stared at me. Without the layers of heavy clothing, he appeared even smaller. Shrunken, and wrinkled as a raisin. He epitomized the term wizened. He looked as old as you could get without being mummified. When he laughed, however, he revealed a set of perfect white teeth. Good living or good dental work, I couldn't begin to guess.

"What I want not matter. What you need is what you do here on farm."

What I needed was to talk to Grace. "Do you have wifi?" I asked him.

His cackles of amusement echoed in my mind for a long while afterward.

Six: Guru June

Mack had said I would be doing what I needed to do. Apparently, this consisted of shoveling shit, fetching well water, and doing laundry in a tub full of his used bath water. He had a bathtub, apparently, while I went without.

Gaman, I told myself.

I was also responsible for gathering up ripe produce, then cleaning off the dirt and manure. Plus any of the other daily duties Mack decided he didn't want to do. He milked the cow and the mature female goats. He fed the animals. Every once in a while, he made goat cheese. Most days he took off in his golf cart, either to the market or to visit neighbors. He returned with fresh eggs, rice, sometimes a whole fish. At night, he made me dinner.

So there was that. He was *almost* like a personal chef.

He made hearty meals for me, but he would eat only a small dish of steamed yams with garlic and a bowl of miso soup. While he watched me gobble up the full plates of hot food he served me, Mack sipped his burdock tea and talked about women. Apparently, what *he* needed to do was go into town as often as possible, get drunk in the bars there, and get himself laid.

Or so he claimed.

"Marriage like movie trailer. All good parts in first few minutes," he said when I asked why he didn't have a wife around to help him with the farm.

After a meandering discourse on the joys of pay by the hour girlfriends, he said, "I try to be a good man, but all that comes of trying is I feel more guilty."

I must have looked surprised at his use of complete sentence structure because he flashed me a sly grin. "Line from poem by Ikkyu. Favorite Zen poet."

Oh.

Then he said, "Zen require aimless nonaction. Spontaneous. Only with drink and girl can man practice full on Zen."

Right. What a lame excuse for being a sleaze.

Some nights while I lay sleepless on my cold futon, watching the moon rise outside my window, the sky filling with stars, ugly thoughts would creep into my mind. Had Mack talked the way he did to me to my sweet Grace? She'd said the training was a nightmare. Could he have...

No, that would never happen. I trusted Martin. The man was bizarre but totally aboveboard and single-mindedly devoted to his cause. He wouldn't let young women come here if anything funny was going on.

Still, I wanted desperately to talk to Grace. But I couldn't, I was trapped inside a pseudo Zen koan. Mack said there were no cell towers close enough to receive a signal at the farm. He had wifi, a cable line of some kind I imagined, but he told me I couldn't use it until he gave me permission. "When you in real need, you use," were his reassuring words of grand Zen wisdom.

Great. Just great. How come dying of boredom and aching from loneliness didn't indicate real need? Not every man goes to town and hires himself a whore.

One night after I had been at the farm for more than two weeks, Mack ladled out a bowl of cabbage soup with some kind of weedy sprouts floating in it. It smelled rank. When I picked up my spoon, my guru didn't sit down. He didn't pour himself a cup of tea, and join me while I ate. Instead, he pulled on a wool hat with ear flaps and reached for his ratty scarf.

I looked at him quizzically.

"Going to town," he said. "Man have need. Time for visit to loose lady waiting to satisfy." A goofy leer lit up his wrinkled face. "Surprise for you on top shelf," he said over his shoulder. When he opened the door, cold mountain air rushed in. "You work hard. Good worker."

He giggled, then shut the door behind him.

When I heard the cart spin out on the gravel, I waited for another minute or two to hear if he might return. He didn't, so I pushed the smelly soup away and jumped up. Man have need, all right. I was going to hack into his wifi connection and connect with Grace.

Sometime later, I stood up from Mack's desk and switched off the desk lamp. With a loud groan of frustration, I abandoned the attempt to hack his laptop after being defeated in multiple attempts to guess his password. My soup still sat on the table, cold now and even more smelly.

Discouraged and shaking with hunger, I decided to help myself to something less stinky. So I scavenged through the refrigerator and combed the kitchen shelves until I found what I wanted.

Screw Zen. Screw Mack. Screw *mottainai.* There was always sake. Oh yes. I'd also found a chunk of cheese, as well as a package of rice cakes. I fixed myself a civilized snack, pouring a generous glass of sake. I didn't bother to heat it.

If Mack gave me any shit, I would just say, *I try to be a good man, but all that comes of trying is I feel more guilty.*

Contemplating saying this to Mack made me laugh.

Two glasses of sake later, stretched out on his rug with his wood stove pumping out the heat, I felt good for the first time since I'd boarded the plane in Fort Lauderdale. Maybe because of the toasty fire, and maybe because the carpet was heated. Yes, Mack had himself an electric rug. He re-used his bathwater for laundry and fertilized his food with his animals' waste, but he didn't skimp on home heating. Most Japanese people had no insulation, no heat. They wore all their winter clothes to bed. Even having a wood stove was a rare luxury in this part of the world. But my guru *needed* the warmth.

Scoffing to myself, I contemplated my own needs. Maybe what I really needed was to call it quits. Go in search of a neighbor, get a lift to the train station, make my way back to Tokyo and home. Yeah, maybe what *I* needed was to return to civilization, where I could see my girlfriend, sleep in my own bed, and be warm at night. Maybe what *I* needed was to do something besides my guru's menial chores.

What I needed.

Suddenly I remembered Mack's "surprise." I stood up and, feeling quite drunk, shuffled over to the bookshelf where he had indicated leaving something for me.

A sheet of paper sat atop a pile of books on Zen. Books Mack had offered to loan me, books I hadn't bothered to borrow. Why? Because I wasn't serious about learning all I could from the training. I was just trying to get by. Why had Mack even said I was working hard? I knew I wasn't. I was doing what was expected of me. Nothing more.

On the paper, in a hard to decipher scrawl: "Lone moon, no clouds/we stumble through the night. —Ikkyu." Below that: "*Mu.* Nothing. *Wu-wei*, Zen for no-thing. No action."

Huh?

And then, there it was. The final word of his cryptic message: "Password."

In a head buzzing with sake, I could hear Mack's annoying giggle. Joke was on me. As usual.

Scowling now, I hurried back to the laptop and typed in the two foreign words. Yup, sure enough, that was the password. A Zen koan, one that had been solved.

The connection was slow, but it worked. Minutes later, I scanned my traffic jam of emails. I only paused to open the ones from Grace. Work was busy. The apartment was wonderful. She was getting spoiled, living in such luxury. She missed me.

She missed me.

I set up Skype and messaged her, and she answered right away. "Took you all this time to get access to his computer?" she teased. "He gave me the password on the second day."

"Braggart," I said, my eyes tearing up with some weird kind of drunken sappy desire. "You must've charmed him." *Sharmed,* I think I said.

Arching one fine eyebrow, she said, "I see you found the sake. He plants bottles for you to steal, you know." She leaned forward, her sweet face looking so concerned my heart felt warm and gooshy. "Are you okay? Is it bad?"

"Not so bad. Just boring. I don't see how being a drudge for some old farmer guy will make me less desirous. In fact," I said, stopping to take an obvious peek at her lovely breasts. She was wearing a man's undershirt, the kind they call wife beaters. No bra. A spinnaker of drool lowered itself from my open mouth. "In fact, I want everything now. In vast quantities. Especially you."

51

Her face changed then, the warmth of her smile buoying my poor heart. "You're just going through withdrawal. It will pass. Has he taken you to the river yet? The lakes?"

I sighed. My desire for her wasn't going to go away. I knew that now. "No. I've been too busy cleaning up after him while he stands around watching all the incredible vegetables grow. Somehow, in that weedy garden of his, everything he plants comes out healthy. Vibrant, and ridiculously huge."

She nodded. "No-till farming is the way to go. His soil is rich. He plants everything carefully, allowing his crops to enrich the soil in cycles. No fertilizers required. No weeding either because the weeds help keep the bad insects away from his crops. Mack practices no work farming. Which is why everyone goes to study with him. Who doesn't want better results from less work?"

"Yeah, but he makes *us* do all his work." I was whining, but it was true.

She nodded again. "You got it."

Even drunk, I got it. Another koan solved.

We chatted for a while about Mottainai, the latest in office politics, and the recent unsettled weather. I'd missed a week of violent thunderstorms. I could smell the hot wet asphalt, the ozone tang after lightning strikes. Nobody did thunderstorms like South Florida.

"Will he let me use the computer again?" I asked. "Or is he

going to change the password after this?"

She shrugged. "Who knows with Mack? But you should get off the farm for a bit and check out the local sights. Tomorrow, after the chores are done, tell him you need to get out and about. There's lots to choose from. Mountains. More than thirty lakes. The gorgeous bay."

"Yeah, I'd really like that," I said.

"You have to tell him what you need. Otherwise, it won't happen. But he'll probably be in a generous mood after his night out. He's malleable after he's been a bad boy." Her beautiful eyes twinkled.

My heart lurched around my chest. "He didn't try to…with you…?"

"Oh gosh, no," she said, shaking her head. Her pretty hair fell softly around her shoulders. "He's not like that. He's an old man, and a decent one. The older Japanese men, they had certain customs with wives, and with other women. I can't imagine who these women he sees are, actually. Maybe I don't want to imagine."

I agreed with that. As we continued to talk, my heart gradually settled down. But I couldn't deny it, I was a lot in love with this woman.

At the end of our conversation, Grace said, "I hope you get to explore the area soon." She sighed wistfully. "The sea is so beautiful. Wish I was there to enjoy it with you."

Me too.

After we said our good nights, I read through my email and surfed the internet. Everything in the news seemed to have nothing to do with me. It all felt so unreal.

Only Grace and my life on the farm seemed real anymore.

I shut down the computer, clicked off the rug heat, and cleaned up the mess I'd made. Washed and dried the dishes, rearranged the desk, straightened the room. I had to compost the uneaten soup. Back in my dark little hut, stretched out on the floor, I slept like a baby. Or maybe I simply passed out like an old drunk.

When I greeted my host the next morning, he snickered. Did I look that hungover? He said, "The mirror has two faces, both haggard."

I said, "Ikkyu?"

He shook his head carefully, like it was made of glass. "No, Bukowski."

We both laughed a little, partners in our self-inflicted suffering. But when I asked him later that afternoon if we might take a drive to the water, one of the many local lakes, the river, the sea that was so close we could taste the salt on the morning breeze, he frowned at me. "Not what you need."

"And what's that?" I countered, a fiery shot of anger rising to flush my face.

"Chop more wood for stove," he replied. He pointed to the barn where an axe had been propped against the door. "You use up wood.

Mottainai. Time for fire not summer. You need replace my wood."

So I'd lit a fire, so what? The days were comfortable, the June sun warm enough that I could strip down to a tee shirt. But because of the mountains and the tall trees that shaded the farm, night came early. And at this altitude, the nights were cold. Mack had the *kotatsu*, the rug, maybe an electric blanket on his bed so he could stay warm. I had none of that to help me through the night.

But what could I say? I was here to learn how to not be so wasteful. He was right to accuse me of reverting to old habits the moment his back was turned. So, emitting only an annoyed sigh, I did as instructed. I hefted the axe over one shoulder and walked toward the woods.

"Go deep. No apple tree," Mack called after me. Then he laughed.

Screw him, I thought. Screw this whole damn summer.

I had never chopped wood in my life. But morons chopped wood. President Bush chopped wood. How hard could it be? As I walked along, I looked for solid branches within easy reach and larger trees that had fallen to the ground on their own. I wasn't going to cut down a live tree, nor would I climb one. Instead, I would choose discarded wood, recycling it for Mack's stove.

Maybe I was learning about the no work way of life after all.

The tall pines were majestic, the beeches thick with foliage, the sky a patchwork quilt through the uppermost branches. I hiked along, enjoying the scenery.

The woodsy silence around me was broken by a loud squeal. An animal chattered right above my head. When I looked up, a small monkey stared back, his dark eyes suspicious. He tossed something to the ground, then scampered upward into the leafy greenery to hide.

Cool.

I had been careful on my way into the woods to make sure I traveled due north so I could easily backtrack, but when I was done collecting a decent amount of branches, I realized I had nothing to carry them home in. I arranged the armload of firewood along with the axe across my extended arms, then began the slow trek back.

Darkness had seeped in, enveloping the woods around me. Even though I was pretty sure it was still late afternoon, I couldn't see very well. I tried not to panic, but I was scared of getting lost. Knowing Mack, he'd never send out a search party, instead letting me learn how to be Zen while freezing to death in the forest.

Every once in a while, I heard rustlings coming from the brush behind me. Bears, I was sure of it. Or wild boar. I didn't want to run into either animal. No thanks.

I trekked on, trying to be chill. Was I lost? Then I heard the monkey chattering. I headed toward the chirruping. If it was the same animal, that meant I was probably going in the right direction. I breathed a sigh of relief when I spotted him, sitting on a long branch.

My own live signpost.

When I passed under, he gave me a hard stare. Like he was both angry and frighteningly human. Then he chucked something at me. *Bonk!* A piece of hard fruit of some kind hit me on the head.

I startled, clutching my armload, then laughed out loud. As he scuttled up the tree, I thanked him for the assist.

As I moved ahead, the woods grew even darker. I continued to hear rustling noises and what I was pretty sure were wild animal sounds. At one point, I stood frozen in place, listening to something crash through the brush ahead. When I peered out from behind a wide fir tree, a small furry animal the size of a mink stood a few feet away, nosing about in the undergrowth. I recognized the white-faced marten from the guidebooks on Japanese fauna and flora.

For a few minutes, I watched it burrow and scratch at the dirt. Then it glanced my way and noticed me. I didn't move. The black eyes studied me for a moment before it stuck its nose in the air, turned around and wandered away.

Soon after that, I broke through the thick brush and walked out into the clearing at the edge of the orchard. The sky was both navy blue and orange as the final rays of the setting sun streamed over the farmland. Boy, was I grateful to see my crummy little hut.

Exhausted from the exertion and a numbing terror, I promised myself I would back off the fire building. I loved seeing wild animals, but I didn't want to get lost in the woods again.

By the time I went over to Mack's for dinner, my mood had sunk along with the sun. I missed civilization, the comforts of home. Living away from all the pleasures and excitements of modern life like this was so hard. Sometimes it was stressful or scary, but mostly it was boring.

Dinner consisted of squid and steamed greens with daikon radish. Everything tasted delicious. When I was full, I told him about the monkey with the perfect aim.

Mack laughed. "Japanese macaque, little devil. You lucky he not take shit on your head."

Yeah, that was me, Mr. Lucky.

I must have been frowning because Mack said, "So serious! You good worker. But cultivate too much self-eradication." I stopped stirring my tea. What the heck did he mean by that? He smiled at me, an odd expression in his eyes. "Look in mirror for one true face," he said.

Right. Whatever. I sipped my tea, said nothing. I'd decided guru wisdom bored me to distraction.

After I cleaned the dishes and swept the floor, I left. There was nothing to do but stare at the cold bare walls of my barren abode. How would I be able to stand another ten weeks of this? I was already more miserable than I'd ever been in my life.

Days later, when I googled the Bukowski quote, I found Mack had lied about the attribution.

Typical guru. All smoke and mirrors, those guys.

Seven: Distractions

On the nights when Mack left me alone so he could gallivant with the town drunks and whores, I too did my best to party. I didn't stoke up the fire, not anymore, but I did make myself at home at his place.

First I would prepare a feast from the foods he never served me like rice cakes spread with goat cheese, pickled plums, salted nuts and other packaged snacks. Then I would root out a fresh bottle of sake. There always seemed to be an unopened bottle around. I'd run the lights, switch on the computer, catch up on email, Skype with Grace.

As the summer days grew longer and, I figured, my host became increasingly bored with me, he escaped to the finer things in life more often. By mid-July, he was going into town every other night.

On one of those lost evenings, I was already four cups deep into Mack's sake stash when Grace interrupted my drunken monologue. She was smiling, but there was an edge to her voice that made me sit up straighter.

"Why do you think he lets you hang out in his house like this, drinking up his wine?"

I shrugged, and tried to change the subject back to what I would do to her soft beautiful flesh when I was released from my Asian purgatory and returned to the real world.

She frowned, shaking her head and tossing her shiny hair. God, I missed being with her. She felt to me like a beautiful projection from another reality. I wanted to smell her hair, to be able to touch her naked skin, and...

"Greer, listen to me. He is allowing you to fail by tempting you with worldly distractions."

I laughed at that. "*He's* the one enjoying all the distractions. He's out almost every night now. Drinking, and seeing women."

Her lips arched upward in a knowing smile. "*You're* drinking. And you're *seeing* a woman."

I began to protest, then stopped. She was right. I was in my cups, sweet talking my lover. Mack had tricked me. The minute he wasn't there, standing guard over me, I'd reverted to my former slack-moral self. Instead of focusing on my learning process, I'd allowed myself to be tempted. How weak. And Mack was leaving me alone with the wine and the food and the internet simply to show me just how weak I really was.

The realization hit me like a blow to the head. The training program, the journey I'd embarked on, the work here and the life of less waste, all of it had been a farce.

"*Mottainai,*" I said with a groan.

Grace nodded. "Right. But don't freak out. I fell for it too. Everyone does. He makes it too easy."

That he did.

She went on, soothing me with her calm, caring voice. "You just need to regroup, Greer. Then you can beat him at his own game. Next time he goes into town, go ahead and stay at his place. Take advantage of the electricity, the *kotatsu*, the rug. But turn on the reading lamp, and do something you really need to do. Read his books. I was so lonely, but I finally got a grip and explored his library."

I could do that. "All right, that's what I'll do." I sighed, looking her in the eye. "Anyway, getting wasted like this and talking to you, it feels good for the moment. But overall, it isn't helping. I mean it isn't helping me miss you any less."

She put her hand on the screen and so did I. We touched hands, sort of. Like I was in prison and she was there for visiting hour. Except she'd once been on the other side of the glass. And she'd made it through, and promised me it was worthwhile.

I trusted Grace. So that night was a turning point in my journey.

The long summer days still could have a chill to them, the sun sometimes stingy and scarce. My mornings were spent doing the same menial tasks, with longer hours in the garden harvesting the ripe crops. Since Mack tended the animals and the food seemed to grow itself, actual farming took up a minimal amount of time. After chores and a lunch picked straight from the garden and eaten in a salad, my day's duties were usually done. I had grown stronger, more sure of myself, and I could accomplish the daily tasks efficiently and with little exertion.

In my free time, I explored the area surrounding the farm. I spent long afternoons hiking the outskirts of the Ou Mountains, scouting for interesting wildlife. I discovered a gorgeous deep blue lake, where I braved the cold and went skinny dipping. I almost froze my man parts off. This water was nothing like the bathtub water off Florida's southern coastline. But since I'd been bathing by splashing myself with well water for weeks, the lake was a welcome change. A quick swim there became a regular part of my routine. I jumped in every few days, always with a joyous yodel.

I picked bouquets of wildflowers, watched colorful birds seeking food and mates, even spied on a couple of playful bear cubs roughhousing under a red pine. I made a quick exit, however, to be safe. I was pretty sure the protective mother would not be in a friendly mood if she returned and spotted me hovering near her cubs.

On the nights Mack took the golf cart into town, I cleaned his kitchen and swept the floor, then hung around until very late, reading. I took Grace's suggestion, devouring the books in Mack's library. He had quite a few titles in English, obviously intended for those of us who came to the farm for training. I started with an introductory text on Buddhism, then a kids' book about Shinto animism, that is, the belief that material things have a kind of spirit. By the end of the month, I'd moved on to the Zen philosophers. I read about Ikkyu and his hedonistic lifestyle. And another famous poet, Ryokan, who loved to get drunk and play silly games with the local children. These men were so real, so full of spirit and humanity. Nothing like the serious, distant, authoritarian gurus I had imagined.

These ancient gurus were more like Mack.

One misty afternoon after I delivered a pail of well water to Mack's house, he invited me inside. I followed him over to the *kotatsu,* where he sat down to drink his burdock tea. "You work hard," he said, nodding approvingly. "Good worker. No self-eradicate."

I didn't know what to say so I said nothing. The house was too warm and it smelled bad, like something was rotting.

"Take drive with me?" he asked, his dark eyes dancing.

Would I like to be let out of prison, you mean? This was what flashed through my mind.

After I told him yes, I would love to, Mack stood up. He seemed lighter, almost see-through, his thin frame hollowed out. "We go coast. Fog on Sea of Japan very beautiful."

The coast was miles away. I wondered if the electric cart would make it there and back without recharging. But really, I didn't care if it didn't. Anything was better than another day just like the last one. Just like the last fifty-nine.

When I came out of my hut, I wore a bathing suit under my jeans. I had on a hoodie and carried my jacket. I didn't know what to expect so I was prepared for any weather. Mack had pulled up in the golf cart, and he sat there waiting. He was bundled in layers of rag-tag clothing and wore his wool cap. The mist had turned into a steady drizzle.

Maybe we wouldn't get the chance to sunbathe, but I was excited anyway.

We sped off the property and onto the dirt road that led to the main drag. As we rolled along, my host was quiet, contemplative. After a few minutes, I realized I could smell the same strange odor his house had taken on. A spoiled fruity aroma. Like he'd been overripe and composted. I wondered if it was from drinking too much booze. Or the smell of winnowing body flesh.

When we came to a fork in the road, Mack said, "You pick."

I laughed. How would I know the right way?

"It's logical: when you are not going anywhere, any road is the right one." He grinned at me.

"Ikkyu," we said in unison.

No cars were in sight, nothing coming our way from either direction. Nobody was liable to either, it seemed. Without thinking, I pointed to one of the two narrow roads. I chose the one that led in a more easterly direction. I imagined both would take us to the sea. Another one of the master's tricks.

Or not. Whatever, I was enjoying the scenery. Lush woods broken up by small pastures with grazing cows or mules. An occasional horse, sometimes flocks of goats. Neat wood houses surrounded by yards boasting a profusion of flowers and vines, hearty plants and bushes. Blackberries and tomatoes, salad greens growing wild. Nobody would go hungry in this region of Japan.

Mack saw me looking at all the produce, much of it ripe for the picking. "Neighbors learn from me. No work farming. Let nature feed you." He seemed proud of his accomplishments. "They give me egg, fresh catch fish, mackerel, sardine. Sometime make mochi rice cake for me." He turned to face me, his black eyes sad. "They will miss me."

Miss him? He wasn't going anywhere. Was he?

I hesitated to ask what he meant. Mack was so private. I didn't want to be rude and overstep the allotted amount of intimacy. So I said, "They will have to learn to understand the potency of emptiness."

Mack recognized the quote from his own books. He smiled at me. "Good. You do good work."

By the time I smelled the briny richness of the sea, we were already there. The mist had thickened to a dense fog that muffled the sound of waves on rocks, the relentless hiss and suck that seemed to be so many feet below us. Mack drove more slowly because it was increasingly difficult to see the road. We seemed to be the only ones on it, perhaps for this very reason.

The wind was cold, the sun completely absent. Inside my head, I snickered about wearing a bathing suit. Foolish American tourist.

As we chugged up the steep incline, Mack was silent. Suddenly, he pulled over to the side of the road and parked. Without looking at me, he said, "*Mottainai* mean trash, but trash can have value. Waste *not* wasted? That worth something. Worth changing. If you choose low waste path, many riches to be made. US export toxic waste to Asia, ship to poor countries. This *mottainai.*"

It was the most elaborate thing the man had ever said to me. I sat there in awe as he continued, the fog holding us together in a kind of eerie suspension of reality.

"You good worker. Go home, teach zero waste. Make big plan, build empire on no waste."

Oh sure, that would be easy to pull off. I said, "And how do you propose I do that, Mack?"

He giggled. "*Wu-wei.*" He giggled louder, said it again. He slapped his knee, laughing harder.

Huh? Did he mean do nothing? Non-action? I wondered whether he'd lost it or if this was yet another tease. Another one of his Zen tricks.

He turned to look at me then, still laughing. His breath smelled like overripe plums. Had he been drinking? "Lone moon no clouds, we stumble through the night." He shrugged. "You find way."

Typical guru. So full of practical advice.

The fog blinded us to anything beyond a few feet from the electric cart. My disappointment was tinged with anger. "So, Mack, we aren't going to be able to actually *see* the sea today, are we?"

His smile faded. "Look around." He waved a frail arm draped in holey rags. I looked, but there was nothing to see. We sat in a cloud, our visibility limited to one another. "Take good look, Greer. See? Nothing. Just this."

I was taken aback. He'd never used my name before. I said, "Yes. I get it. All there is in this life is ourselves. And that too is nothing but a fleeting dream. A passing away."

I'd done my homework. I got the whole Zen thing. But what to do with it? I couldn't hide on a distant island all my life, eating raw food that grew wild on my little slice of land. Or maybe I could, but I didn't want to. That wasn't the life I needed. "So what are you saying I should do, Mack? I mean, what do *you* think I should do with my life?"

He stared at me. For a brief moment, we were both silent. The crash of the waves on the rocks grew increasingly louder.

In an instant, the fog thinned and the remaining mist lifted. I could see we were parked at the very edge of the road, only a few yards from a sharp drop-off. Rainbows sparkled in midair where the moisture was quickly evaporating.

Mack broke the silence. "Our lives are like seaweed, floating on the water's edge."

Almost everything he'd been saying I had also read in his books, the ones by the Zen poets. Did the man have nothing original to say to me?

With the fog gone, the sun felt hot on my skin. I tried not to feel so angry. After all, now I could enjoy the view. The waves were amazingly loud, roaring and smashing against the rocks below.

In one smooth motion, Mack climbed out of the cart. He walked swiftly to the edge of the cliff. There was no guardrail. He peered down.

I climbed out of the cart too, excited to see the Sea of Japan. At this elevation, the afternoon sun felt very close. The rays beat down hard, burning through my heavy clothing. I yanked my sweatshirt over my head and turned to toss it in the back of the golf cart. I swear, I only took my eyes off him for a couple of seconds.

When I looked around again, he was gone.

Eight: One Journey Ends, Another Begins

That's when the real nightmare began.

Working on the farm, cleaning the outhouse and shoveling manure, being hungry and eating raw vegetables out of the ground, sleeping in a cold hut on a hard futon, the weeks of training had not been dream living. But it sure seemed like a lost dream after I ran over to the cliff edge and looked down. Because all I saw was the wild raging sea a hundred feet below, the harsh waves smashing themselves against a steep wall of jagged black rocks.

There was no sign of Mack. No body, no giggling guru hiding just below eye level. Nothing but sheer drop-off rock ledge, jutting boulders, all the way down, down, down to the roaring sea.

Nothing else. *Mu.*

Moments later, the fog closed in on me again. And I stood there, all alone in a nightmare of sudden, drastic, catastrophic loss.

Great, just great. Now what?

I ran back to the golf cart and started it up. I would return the way we'd come, stopping at the first farmhouse I saw, begging the people there for help.

The rain held off but the fog clung to the mountainside, slowing progress. At first I drove fast, but I kept veering too close to the edge of the road. Each time, my pounding heart lurched up into my throat and, with a yelp of abject fear, I steered the cart back on track. My poor psyche couldn't take it, so I rode the brakes, staying away from the sides of the narrow and steeply declining road.

My mind continued to race at top speed. There was no way anyone could survive a drop like that. No way. Had Mack fallen? Had he jumped? Did he commit suicide? Why would he do that? Would the authorities be able to find his body? Would they think I was at fault?

As my mind zoomed ahead of the slow moving cart, the fog around me gradually diminished to a thin mist. The tall evergreen trees began to take shape in the fuzzy afternoon light. When the sun broke through, the sudden warmth flooded my shaking body. This had a calming effect on me, allowing my mind to ease its anxiety-fueled charge to all the worst case scenarios.

The Zen reading I had done rippled through my thoughts, releasing the unchained emotions I was experiencing. I let the horror and the fear leak away and what was left was this: a need for purposeful but unattached action. As I drove down the quiet road, a clear thought appeared in my mind, replacing the fear driven images. Mack was gone. The reality was just that simple. Mack was *gone*.

And what would he have expected of me? That was obvious. He would want me to be clear-minded and chill. To do what needed to be done and no more. Not to overwork the situation, but to let it unfold. Let it unfold as naturally as possible.

The road evened out as I left the mountainside and approached the surrounding farmland. I knew what I would do next. I would get some kind of assistance, and in its time the situation would be resolved. Everything would be as it was supposed to be. My life was like the seaweed, floating along the water's edge. There was nothing for me to worry about. It was, indeed, *mu.*

The first house I spotted sat back from the road, a wooden cottage with a rust colored roof. I pulled in the dirt drive and rolled to a stop by the front door. An old woman had come outside at the sound of an approaching visitor, and she stood waiting for me on the porch. In her thin arms, she held a straw basket, the contents covered with a white cloth napkin.

"I need help," I said to the woman, hoping she would somehow understand. "You speak English? It's an emergency."

After giving me a slow bow, she walked out to where I was parked. Then she reached out to hand me the basket.

"No, no, I need to use your phone," I told her, miming the act of holding a receiver to my ear. "Make call to police. Get help."

She smiled at me, setting the basket in the rear of the cart. Then she said, "Tamaki." She bowed again and turned away. Even as I called after her, she continued on her way and soon was back inside her house.

I lifted up the napkin. The basket was full of large eggs. The colors varied from yellow to tan, brown to pure white. They smelled like fresh hay and they were still warm.

When I pulled up to the next farmhouse, an old man rushed toward me from his fields, speaking in Japanese. I understood nothing, and he didn't seem to know what I was trying to communicate either. Sign language proved wholly ineffective. After giving me a wide toothless smile, he hurried over to his sagging porch and returned with an extension cord. This he plugged into the golf cart.

He grinned at me, nodding repeatedly as he proceeded to charge up the battery. Talking rapidly and using both hands for emphasis, he said whatever he had to say. I heard the word *tamaki* again, and wondered what it meant.

He left me standing there while he went inside his house. He soon returned with a glass of bright green liquid, which he delivered along with a long stream of unintelligible chatter. He kept on smiling, nodding and pointing, waiting for me to accept the drink.

I sipped a little of the cool liquid, reflective. A sweet tea. It tasted delicious so I nodded and smiled at my host.

These were Mack's neighbors. They obviously recognized his golf cart, so they were treating me the way they would normally respond to him. There was nothing I could do to inform them of the crisis that had befallen Mack.

Later on, when the old man unplugged the power cord, I bowed to him before starting up the cart. During my time waiting for the charge, I'd wandered the perimeter of the man's farm, thinking. I'd decided the best plan was to return to Mack's house and contact the authorities from there. I could use his computer.

The truth was, I had no other choice.

Late afternoon sun lingered, warming, lulling me. By the time I turned down the dirt road that led to Mack's farm, I felt oddly peaceful. Whatever happened would be what happened. The sky had lit itself up, the setting sun a blazing orange. In the distance, hundreds of apple trees were on fire. The orchard was in bloom.

I parked the cart by the barn and stopped at the well for water. I filled the bucket and carried it to my hut, where I washed up by the front door. Then I fetched an additional bucket to make myself a pot of strong tea. If the Japanese authorities were anything like the cops at home, it was going to be a long night of questions and explanations.

I went inside Mack's house to prepare the tea. I was not worried. Somehow, I would stumble on. *Gaman.* I would do whatever I could, and I would make it through the night.

Seated at his desk, I turned on the laptop. I would contact the police station in Fukamura, ask them what I should do next. Then I would contact Grace. And Martin.

When the door swung open, I looked up with a start. Mack walked in. He was moving slowly. Grabbing his belly, he glanced at me and grimaced. "Take big dump. Run too fast, cramp bad."

I gaped at him. I couldn't believe it, he'd duped me again. The nightmare had been induced. Just another one of Mack's stupid tricks.

The man was insufferable.

In the kitchen, he reached in a low cupboard and rummaged around, pulled out a green bottle. He put it on the table along with two glasses. He clasped his stomach again as he dropped down to sit on the floor pillow. "Don't sit with mouth open like fish. Come drink," he ordered.

Drink? *Drink?* I wanted to kill the man, not clink glasses with him.

Too angry to speak, I remained silent, grappling with my temper. While he filled the glasses with an amber liquid, I shut down the computer and stood up. I switched off the lamp, collected my mug of tea. I was moving as if in a trance. Mack wasn't dead. He'd pretended to jump, then taken a shortcut home. The neighbors all knew there was no emergency, so of course they didn't react to my anxiety because they'd seen it all before. He must have pulled the same stunt on every poor sap who trained at the farm.

The lousy bastard.

I imagined hot steam shooting from my ears as I joined him at the *kotatsu*. The man was a Zen monster. I was sick of his shit. I would leave in the morning. I'd had enough of his pointless head games.

He slid one glass across the table and held up his own, as if to toast me. He drank his down and poured himself another. I recognized the yellow label. Jameson. Irish whiskey.

I didn't drink. I didn't move or speak. My temper was settling down, it was almost under control again, when he looked me in the eye and said, "Congratulations, Greer Grassi. You've done very well. There's no need to stay another month. Your training period is complete. You may return to the US whenever you wish."

I stiffened. My mind reeled. What the *hell?* The man spoke *perfect English?*

He cocked his head, assessing my level of ire. Then he nodded to my untouched drink. "I'm surprised you didn't break into the whiskey while I was out all those nights. Why drink sake when you can knock back the Irish?"

That's when I lost it.

My rant was extremely loud and accompanied by bouts of vigorous pounding on the table. Mack held his glass in one hand so his drink wouldn't spill while I yelled at him about everything from his lame accommodations to his terrible sense of humor. I accused him of tourist abuse and taking advantage of foreigners to shirk his own responsibilities. I called him the Tom Sawyer of Japan. He smirked at that. But he frowned deeply when I said he was a poser and a phony.

He finished the second glass of whiskey, then set his glass on the table with a pointed glance at my fist. As if to say, *don't do that anymore, I'm tired of holding this glass in my hand.*

He must've seen my eyes blaze up again because he grabbed the glass and reached for the bottle. "Drink, my friend. Relax. Everything is going to be okay."

It was his barroom *don't worry, be happy* attitude that set me off that time.

Soon, however, I got tired of yelling. He just sat there, drinking, a bemused expression on his pruney face. Eventually, my rage settled into a disgruntled exhaustion and I shut up. I drank some whiskey, let it burn down my sore throat to my empty stomach.

After a while, he slid the bottle across the table and I refilled my glass.

"Why?" I managed to ask, once my bloodstream was sufficiently suffused with soothing booze heat. "Why the ruse, the poor Asian wise man farmer act?"

He shrugged. His shoulders were hunched and, sitting there staring at me, he looked smaller now than ever. He glanced away and sighed. "You Westerners seem to need a goddam Hollywood production to motivate you to simply use your own common sense."

That was true. I smiled sheepishly.

He continued. "When Martin's dad found me years ago, I was working as an agrobiologist in a corporate lab in Cambridge. Massachusetts, not England," he explained. "I grew up in New York, got educated in Boston. Then, armed with a PhD from Oxford in plant biology, I moved back to the US to work in research. But I was already disillusioned. Too many dead ends created by the ivory tower of academia. I harbored this crazy vision of moving to a rural location and testing out my theories myself. Theories about farming without fertilizers, revitalizing soil with non-till methods. I'd been working for a decade with worms. Vermiculture with *Eisenia foetida* and *Lumbricus rubellus.* Species that can compost soil far better than anything humans create in a lab."

Did he tell all the trainees this story? Was it more bullshit to twist my mind in another Zen knot? I sipped the whiskey, which helped to relax my anxiety. And I tried to open my mind to what Mack had to say.

"I'd found out which weeds would foster plant growth, and which insects were protective for various individual crops. I believed I could run a productive farm with minimal labor. A self-running organic farm located off the grid, away from all the nonsense and pollution of civilization. I cannot tell you how much this appealed to me at the time."

I understood. Escapist fantasy has an allure for many young men. It had brought me halfway around the world to his farm as well.

Mack said with a shrug, "Martin's a weird guy, but he is quite brilliant and big hearted. So was his father. Martin Senior made a serious killing in the financial sector, and he wanted to do good things with his windfall. He came to see me because he was interested in organic farming methods and sustainability. He'd read several of my academic papers and he wanted to learn from me." Mack shrugged again, tilting his head slightly. "I liked the man, you know?"

I did know. I liked Martin as well. I could imagine his father had that same quirky good guy personality.

"He told me he had all this money. He said he would buy me the land I needed to test out my theories. Anyplace I thought would work best. We decided to build the farm at the northern tip of Honshu island. Even though I spent time in Kyoto as a child, visiting my relatives, I had never been to Aomori Prefecture. But I had read much about the natural beauty, the pristine resources. One trip and I was hooked. I left my lab position and moved here. That was almost fifty years ago." He looked at his hands, worn and veiny. "It was so beautiful back then, the life I had created. My wife loved it here too."

His *wife?* He'd never mentioned a spouse.

He took a long drink then, his eyes still downcast. "You think I live like Ikkyu, with wild nights spent making poetry with the naked bodies of young whores. I encourage all the trainees to think this. It is part of my guru image." He shook his head, glanced at me, then away. "But the reality of my situation is quite different. On those nights when I go to town, I am there to visit my wife. Sometimes, afterward, I buy a bottle and drink it on the long drive back." He looked at me again, his eyes blank. "She's in a care home and the conditions are terrible. In Japan these days, few young people stay on after their education is complete, especially in the rural areas. All over the country, the population is aging and shrinking. There are so many old people, with not enough younger relatives willing to take them in, and not nearly enough health workers to tend to their needs. It's no good to live too long. *Mottainai*."

An idea seeded itself deep in my mind. I left it alone, not tilling, not fertilizing. Allowing it to grow naturally, on its own, in its own time.

"I'm sorry," I said.

He shrugged, his bony shoulders like small lumps of clay molded into a permanent hunch. "Don't be sorry. Ours was a good life. And when we lived in Cambridge, we had a good life there too. Life has been long, most of it good. But when it is no longer good, it needs to be shed. Like old winter coat on first day of spring."

He was going guru on me again. When I gave him the stink eye, he caught himself and smiled a little, obviously embarrassed. "Sorry. I'm not used to having a real conversation with an American. Even Martin prefers my Zen act."

Poor Mack. How lonely for him to have to play a role all the time.

He set his empty glass on the table. "Greer, I want you to know that your visit will serve as my final training session. I plan to harvest the apples on my own this fall, then move into town for the winter. I need to be there for my wife during the time she has left. I can't manage the farm myself anymore. I don't want to." He searched my face. "Next time I pretend to jump off a cliff, I might actually do it. But not until the farm is in good hands. Martin and I are co-owners. I plan to sign the deed over to him."

Well, that would be an interesting development for Mottainai. I wondered if Martin knew about it yet.

Mack fiddled with his glass. "The farm will continue to serve the cause in whatever way Martin decides. It will become his sole property. I will spend my days with my wife, waiting for her to pass on to the next part of her journey."

How long might that take? Was she coherent, mobile? Did she hold his hand, did she even recognize him? I didn't ask. But the seed in my mind germinated. I ignored it and told him, "I said a lot of harsh things earlier—"

He waved his gnarled hand, then reached for the whiskey bottle.

While he topped off my glass, I continued, "—but now I need to say something else. I've learned a lot from you. I've discovered many things about myself during these past two months. I've reordered my priorities, and made some important decisions. Now I know what road I want my life to take."

He glanced at me, a knowing look on his wizened face.

I held up a hand. "I know, I know. Zen has taught me that any road is the right one. I do realize I am not going anywhere, not really. I get that this life is all a Zen dream. But it's *my* goddam dream. And I'm going to make the most of it."

I guess I was drunk. For two months, I'd only imbibed sake. Plus,

I had been psychologically terrorized so was especially vulnerable when I poured on the whiskey.

But Mack was drunk too. So drunk he began to giggle. And that made me laugh.

When I left Mack's for the night, he trailed me to the door. Then, to my surprise, he reached up and grabbed me in a bear hug. His small body was hard as old wood, rigid and yet somehow fragile. More like driftwood.

I hugged him in return.

"Tamaki Murakawa," he said.

I recognized the first word. Both his neighbors had mentioned *tamaki*. "What's that mean?" I asked.

"It's my name." He winked, then bid me goodnight.

In the morning we were both terribly hungover. Without speaking, we went about our routine business and completed the day's chores. While I packed up my duffle, Mack prepared lunch. When I walked into the kitchen, the half-empty bottle of Jameson was on the table. We each managed to gulp down a short shot. Nothing like hair of the dog, the universal hangover remedy.

On the drive to the local train station, the sun peeked out from behind an army of heavy gray clouds. A sliver of bone-white moon hung in the afternoon sky. Mack asked me what my plans were. The seed was still germinating, so I didn't want to discuss it. But I wanted him to know

I was working on something, an idea he had inspired.

I told him I would spend a night in Tokyo, then fly to Boston. "I have relatives in the area I can stay with. I want to do some research while I'm there. It's for an idea I have for a startup. Relating to zero waste," I admitted.

Out of the corner of my eye, I could see he was pleased. He said, "Martin has more money than God. Get him to pony up."

Wise words from a man who had spent decades living off the Handler family's do-gooder welfare. I told Mack I had learned important lessons from my guru about venture capital and how to obtain it. He laughed.

When we pulled into the lot, the train platform was deserted. I climbed out and retrieved my bag. I looked at Mack and he nodded several times. He bowed his head, and I bowed from the waist.

Mack cleared his throat. "If you have need, I would be glad to share some of my most useful contacts at MIT and other academic institutions in the US and elsewhere. There are smart people who like my research. They could be helpful to you."

I thanked him.

He said, "I'm off to see the wife. You have safe travels. I'll look forward to our email correspondence."

I thanked him once more, this time for everything.

He waved that away. Then, with a serious expression on his small face, he leaned toward me. "Wherever you go, be sure to carry the staff of your purpose, and the whiskey jug of your true desire."

"Ryokan?" I asked.

He giggled. "Tamaki Murakawa."

Then he winked at me and sped away, his diminishing figure framed by the towering pines, snowcapped mountains, and a vast blue sky.

Epilogue

Since you are still reading this text, you are now familiar with the concept of *mottainai.* Maybe you are thinking about joining the movement. If so, congratulations. You are about to embark on an incredible and important journey. A life road that will take you in a direction that can improve the state of our fragile world. That will help to make a better life for you, your child, your child's child, and the many generations that follow.

When my flight departed from Tokyo the day after I left Mack's farm, my idea had grown some tender shoots. In Boston, I found the soil I could plant them in. When I returned to Florida a week later, Grace agreed to help me. With Mack's university connections and Martin's financial backing, we would nurture the delicate buds until they blossomed. And then we would spread the seeds worldwide.

Needless to say, I quit my corporate job. My boss wished me luck with my nonprofit venture. He said I was making a serious fiscal mistake, but I could see in his eyes he had respect for me.

Grace and I live in a sunny apartment in Cambridge, just a short walk from the university where we have our offices. Our son will be an only child, and he is the joy of our lives. While he plays nearby at the university preschool, we manage the business. I take care of the technical side, Grace the marketing and what I call schmoozing. She laughs when I tease her about it because she knows networking is her forte. Few can resist her radiant purity, her absolute devotion to the mission of the *mottainai* movement.

Martin operates Mottainai Japan from the farm, where he spends nine months of the year. Every summer when the colleges let out, Grace and I travel there to relieve him of the daily grind. He takes off to attend global events and meetings with other activists, then returns to the US to regroup while we work with the summer trainees. We've built several new huts to allow for groups of visitors and up to six trainees at a time. The lodgings are sparse, but much more comfortable than Grace and I had to endure.

We like to take our trainees on day trips, visiting neighbors and the area sights. We go out on the fishing boats. We hike in the mountains, go swimming in the lakes. I'm especially fond of our picnics at Mutsu Bay, where we sometimes see the wild horses running along the beach. The baby loves going to the Big Buddha. Little Marty speaks almost as much Japanese as he does English, another benefit of spending our summers overseas.

Last June, the day after we arrived at the farm, I drove one of the golf carts into town to visit Mack. I was worried about him. His wife had passed away over the winter. I wouldn't have been surprised if he'd made a beeline for the cliffs. I knocked on the door to his apartment with a heavy heart.

Mack greeted me with a nasty frown. But he was not the least bit suicidal. My visit, he said, was ill-timed. He was busy, he informed me, "entertaining."

He was indeed, and she was quite a lovely woman. I made brief conversation until he gave me the stink eye, then I left. The old trickster still had a few tricks left.

As for the business, we are busy too.

Our first app was designed to connect eaters with good food that would otherwise be wasted, that is, leftover restaurant food made available at day's end at extremely low cost. The program is immensely popular and the income stream from thousands of participating restaurants helps fund our other projects. The end goal is to remake the food supply chain so that it is more efficient. The world produces twenty percent more food than the population actually needs, and about one third of the total production is wasted. Food doesn't get to the people who need it. This is a huge problem, but it is fixable. We just need to be smarter. And more conscious.

We are also involved in the search for new technology, modern solutions to a wide variety of waste problems including agricultural issues, energy alternatives, workplace inefficiency, overpopulation, and end of life choices. Food, energy, work, old age, death—everything can become less wasteful with the right technology and the right consciousness.

Zero waste is the ultimate goal. So we support the university researchers, urban planners, and environmental architects who are developing alternatives to the conventional burial. That is, composting the dead and returning their bodies to the earth. I know, it sounds bizarre, but this is what we mean when we speak about zero waste.

Food, eaten or uneaten, going back to the earth. Us, our lives well lived, going back to the earth.

As the *mottainai* movement spreads the word on reducing food waste, cutting back on consumerism, safeguarding time, working to keep population growth under control, and expanding end of life alternatives, waste consciousness is being raised worldwide. Here are just a few examples of the recent changes in attitude. In parts of Europe, newly formed small businesses collect food waste from supermarkets to distribute to the hungry and impoverished. In northern Africa, farms using no-till techniques grow thousands of acres of organic produce, food that one day might be able to feed the continent. In New Zealand and Australia, home composting is common practice. Canada has passed a liberal right to die law, a model for the US. Even at the end of life, perhaps especially then, we can work to cut back on waste.

Here in the US, the *mottainai* movement is growing. Enthusiasts and vocal proponents are canvassing Congress, lecturing to audiences, and spreading the word on college campuses. There are workshops for employees of large corporations, talks presented to high school classes, and seminars held at city council meetings. The movement is all over the social networks, YouTube, TV.

Mottainai. The message is simple, but not easy to adopt in a postmodern culture that is highly industrialized and consumer-based, with rapidly advancing technology. Change requires a Zen approach, that is, to go ahead and make your own way, enjoy your life journey— but to be careful at the same time to maintain the path for the next guy.

Your life doesn't have to be shallow, dull, a prison or a trap. Your journey can be rich, rewarding, full of adventure and meaning.

The last section of this book provides some simple guidelines you can adopt in order to join the *mottainai* movement. Every journey begins with a first step. And you've already taken that step because you have just finished reading this story.

You have your own story, your own journey, ahead of you. So don't waste any more precious time. If you wish, you can choose to allow the road of your life to take you in a whole new direction.

Kanpai!

A Practical Addendum

"Every great movement must experience three stages:
ridicule, discussion, adoption."
—John Stuart Mill

As you learn the tenets of *mottainai,* you may encounter deep-seated inner resistance, and you might find yourself rejecting or procrastinating in making lifestyle changes. This is perfectly normal. Each individual must forge his or her own path. Remember, if it is defined, it is not Zen.

If you do elect to join the movement, be prepared to face others' derision. Without fail, you will be required to vigorously defend your stance on waste and your choice of lifestyle, and it may take considerable effort to interest others in considering a similar commitment to zero waste. This can be a burden. The personal rewards of doing it yourself, however, are many.

Food waste is the easiest place (or plate) to begin changing your perspective on waste and start altering habits that are wasteful. There are a number of simple things you can do to significantly reduce food waste at home, and thus lighten up your garbage footprint.

Trash is the physical manifestation of our wastefulness. We pay to own stuff, then we pay to have it hauled away when we're done with it. By separating out the food waste, keeping it out of the garbage can, you can reduce the number of garbage bags you lug to the curb. In fact, without rotting food, wastebaskets do not need to be emptied as often. Depending on the number of persons in a household, trash can be limited to a weekly garbage bag. Or less.

Your food scraps can be composted. There are many online resources that can teach you how to do this. The process is simple, not expensive or time consuming. Some cities provide food waste bins and pick up the scraps. All US cities should offer this service.

Food waste does add up. Amounts can be reduced by avoiding impulse food purchases and overbuying. Rather than forcing family members to clean their plates, servings should be appropriate to need, any leftovers saved and creatively reused. No single-serving coffee, bottled water, or the like. The excess waste from such over-packaged products is enormous. Filter your own water, and utilize reusable containers. Keep in mind how it is better to shop more often for fresh foods than to overstock and allow foods to go to waste.

Plan menus in advance. Cook meals at home. Avoid restaurants that over-package takeout. Frequent your local farmers markets and join a farm delivery program (CSA) in your area. Such changes will also serve to improve your eating habits and health, as well as cutting back on food waste. These practices also help to reduce food bills.

Americans dump more than seven pounds of trash per person per day. That's a lot of garbage heading for overcrowded landfills. Amounts are double what we dumped as recently as 1960. The Japanese dump maybe one half or even a third as much as we do. How can that be?

The US economy has become linked to cheap disposables.

Credit based, we have developed a consumer system in which we spend little for our goods but continue to pay off the debt, even after what we've purchased is already in the trash. This makes no sense. In fact, it's dangerously stupid. And wildly unsustainable.

An estimated $50 billion worth of goods is trashed annually. Since we are running out of room in US landfills, trash has become our leading export. We ship our waste, paying others to take it and dispose of it. This includes the toxic waste products we cannot, by law, trash here. Such pollutants are dumped elsewhere, in places where residents are not protected by strict environmental standards for health and safety.

How fair is that?

We need to alter our mindless consumption economy to a system based on product durability and conservation. Public awareness is already creating gradual change. Buying local is trending, and there is increased attention to revitalizing neighborhood economies. There's plenty of work to be done. Congress and city governments need to get involved. Capitalization technology and regulations that encourage change will have to be expanded. What about tax breaks for manufacturers that successfully reduce or reuse packaging? And for corporations that establish take-back programs for products that can be resold?

In the meantime, you can do your part by shopping less often, avoiding unnecessary purchases, and becoming increasingly conscious of what you spend your money on. Ask yourself: Do I need it? How long will it last?

Whatever you buy, it probably has plastic parts or comes packaged in plastic. But plastic is one of our most dangerous pollutants, adding toxic chemicals to air, water, and soil during manufacture, while failing to degrade after disposal. There is so much plastic circulating in our oceans that researchers refer to certain areas as thick with "plastic chowder." The long-term effects of such contamination are unknown.

You can reuse the plastics you receive in packaging, and find substitutes whenever you can. Bring your own reusable bag when you shop. Be creative. Try using something other than plastic bags for your pet waste. If you solved the pet waste problem, you could do your neighbors a huge favor *and* become a millionaire.

Another way to cut back on waste is to shop for clothes and household items at secondhand stores. One person's refuse can be your treasured find. Donate your unwanted stuff, or sell it on consignment. If you receive something you know you have no use for, don't be ashamed to regift.

Recycling works too, but not as well as we might like to think. The problem is that recycling programs encourage us to consume even more by alleviating consumer guilt, making us feel like we're not being wasteful. Some cities have instituted "pay as you throw" collection systems using bins of different sizes. Residents pay less if they make less garbage. Studies show that people will cut back if their garbage bins are smaller in size. What an easy solution! This is a program every city in the US should consider adopting.

In the meantime, do recycle what you can. And remember to compost. Be on the lookout for ways to do with less, and ideas for doing more with your trash. Be aware that the problem of waste is linked to some of the world's most critical issues like climate change, pollution, and the high costs of energy and raw materials. A simple change like cutting down on global waste could serve to usher in an era of increased sustainability, prosperity, and security.

If you are really brave, consider the alternative burial system of recomposition. That is, the composting of dead bodies. This may sound icky, but it is actually the most natural way for all of us to return to the earth. Conventional burials necessitate tons of steel and require hundreds of thousands of gallons of embalming fluid, polluting and using up more land every year. Willing to think (and be buried) outside the box? This new area of ecological research could offer a zero waste solution for an issue we all must face.

One of the greatest resources Americans waste is time. We like to pretend it's unlimited, so we waste time shopping for things we don't need, reading "news" that isn't, stalking the internet and socializing with people we know we should avoid.

Mottainai.

If you regard your time as your most precious resource, however, you can discover more sustainable ways to live in the modern world. Ways that enhance the overall quality of your life and limit your exposure to the toxicities inherent in a culture devoid of real meaning.

You don't need to escape to the mountains in order to accomplish this. It's not necessary to go off the grid and live in a hut, although that may appeal to some. There are practical ways to reduce time wasted on unnecessary activities and energy draining people. You'll need to identify the things you feel most passionate about and spend your free time doing them. And if you believe that your job is a toxic waste of time, you'll need to consider the alternatives. Life is brief and there is a lot of good work that needs to be done. No sense wasting a moment of what we've been given.

Another issue in the waste discussion that is often overlooked is overpopulation. World population is currently more than seven billion and is expected to hit ten billion by the year 2050. Mother Earth cannot support so much human life without serious and widespread detrimental effects. Pollution is increasing steadily as developing countries adopt the wasteful habits of wealthy countries like the US. There's more global poverty, more natural disasters, and diminishing natural resources. And it's going to get worse before it begins to get better.

Too many people, too many problems, too much waste.

The Zero Population Growth (ZPG) movement attained heightened popularity in the US and Europe in the 1960s. The idea was to maintain population numbers at a desirable ratio by matching the replacement fertility rate. That is, the number of births in a country plus the number of new immigrants would be kept equivalent to the number of deaths each year. At the time, many individuals made a voluntary commitment to birthing no more than one child. The movement fell out of favor, however, and the world population has continued to explode.

At the other end of the human lifespan, many developed countries now face problems caused by an aging population. Americans on average live into their eighties. All too often, the final years are spent in doctors' offices as the majority of this population becomes infirm, heavily medicated, and dependent on continual health care. By medicalizing aging, the current system has imposed unsustainable expense. Do people really want to live to be a hundred if their last decades must be spent on government welfare or in costly nursing facilities?

Such questions are personal, yet universal. We are all born, the lucky among us living out our intended lifespan. However, rapidly changing economics, demographics, and technology have reshaped all of our futures. We'll need new, creative solutions to the crises we must face in the US as millions of Boomers reach and live past retirement age. Can the systems we have in place support all the retirees? Will Social Security and other safety nets be adequate? Who will care for all the old folks when they are no longer able to care for themselves?

As the world population reaches a critical mass, we'll all be forced to deal with the consequences.

Mottainai.

Perhaps there are better ways, less wasteful ways, for all of us to live a good life.

You may find the following references, books, and websites to be of interest. There are many resources available that can assist you as you look into reducing waste and adopting a more conscious lifestyle.

Food Waste

Jonathan Bloom, *American Wasteland: How America Throws Away Nearly Half of its Food (And What We Can Do About It),* 2011.

Tristan Stuart, *Waste: Uncovering the Global Food Scandal,* 2009.

Kate Anderson, *Waste Free Kitchen*, 2015.

Dana Gunders, *Waste-Free Kitchen Handbook,* 2015.

Garbage

Edward Humes, *Garbology: Our Dirty Love Affair with Trash,* 2013.

Annie Leonard, *The Story of Stuff,* 2011.

Elizabeth Royle, *Garbage Land: On the Secret Trail of Trash,* 2006.

Susan Strasser, *Waste and Want: A Social History of Trash,* 2000.

Paul Connett, *The Zero Waste Solution: Untrashing the Planet One Community at a Time*, 2013.

Check out these blogs about people who have successfully reduced their waste to unbelievably small amounts:

http://www.trashisfortossers.com/

http://www.zerowastehome.com/

https://myzerowaste.com/

Mottainai

Learn about the history of the Japanese term *mottainai* and current meaning, that is, reduce, reuse, recycle, and respect:

http://www.abc.net.au/radionational/programs/philopherszo ne/avoiding-waste-with-the-japanese-concept-of-'mottainai'/6722720

Wangari Maathai worked as an environmental and political activist; she popularized the term *mottainai* and spread the concept worldwide:

Wangari Maathai, *Replenishing the Earth: Spiritual Values for Healing Ourselves and the Earth,* 2010.

http://www.wehatetowaste.com/mottainai/

Zen, Change, Etc.

Ikkyu, *Crow with No Mouth,* 2000.

John Stevens, *One Robe, One Bowl: The Zen Poetry of Ryokan,* 2006.

Alan Watts, *The Way of Zen,* 1999.

Paul Reps and Nyogen Senzaki, *Zen Flesh, Zen Bones: A Collection of Zen and Pre-Zen Writings,* 1991.

Masanobu Fukuoka, *The One-Straw Revolution: An Introduction to Natural Farming*, 2009.

John Seymour, *The Self-Sufficient Life and How to Live It,* 2009.

Ali Berlow, *The Food Activist Handbook,* 2015.

Paul and Anne Ehrlich, *The Population Explosion*, 1991.

Atul Gawande, *Being Mortal: Medicine and What Matters in the End,* 2014.

Paul Kalanithi, *When Breath Becomes Air,* 2016.

Check out this project to change urban burials:

http://www.urbandeathproject.org/

Food and Nutrition Resources Foundation, Inc. (FNR) is a 501c3 non-profit corporation created in 1976 for the purpose of informing and educating the public about nutrition and health. Currently, FNR focuses on the active support of individuals, communities, and organizations doing good food work in the following areas: organic food production, healthy food availability to schoolchildren and the underserved, resources for the hungry, agricultural sustainability (including vegetarianism, veganism, and animal rights), food justice, and education on healthy eating for a healthy planet.

FNR Foundation
600 NE 20th Avenue
Deerfield Beach, FL 33441
www.fnrfoundation.org

Printed in Dunstable, United Kingdom